Dachshunds

Dachshunds

D. Caroline Coile, Ph.D.

BARRON'S

Acknowledgments

Many Dachshund owners throughout the years have helped greatly with educating me about all things Dachshund. Particular thanks are owed to Jeanette Ringer, Katie Souder, Mary Ann Teal, and Arvind and Joyce deBraganca.

About the Author

D. Caroline Coile, Ph.D., has written 30 books and more than 500 magazine and scientific articles about dogs—and one book about cats. She's also a columnist for *Dog World* magazine and the *AKC Gazette.* Her dog writing awards include the Dog Writers Association of America Maxwell Award (seven times), the Denlinger Award, the Eukanuba Canine Health Award (twice), and the AKC Canine Health Foundation Award (twice). She is the author of the top-selling *Barron's Encyclopedia of Dog Breeds.*

Caroline's research and teaching interests revolve around canine behavior, senses, and genetics. On a practical level, Caroline has lived with dogs all of her life and competed with them for more than 30 years. Her dogs have included nationally ranked show, field, obedience, and agility competitors—who regularly chew up her manuscripts and pull her away from her desk.

All information and advice contained in this book has been reviewed by a veterinarian.

A Word About Pronouns

Many dog lovers feel that the pronoun "it" is not appropriate when referring to a pet that can be such a wonderful part of our lives. For this reason, **Dachshunds** are described as "he" throughout this book unless the topic specifically relates to female dogs. This by no means infers any preference, nor should it be taken as an indication that either sex is particularly problematic.

Photo Credits

Kent Dannen: pages 32, 116, 120, 123, 125, and 150; Kent and Donna Dannen: page 75; Tara Darling: pages 10, 11, 12, 13, 20, 30, 44, 45, 62, 85, 108, 140, 144 (bottom), 154, 156, 159, 161, 162, 164, and 168; Cheryl A. Ertelt: pages 22, 31, 78, 86, 99, 142, and 147; Jean M. Fogle: page 158; Isabelle Francais: pages 15 and 157; Karen Hudson: pages 8, 52, and 88; Daniel/Paulette Johnson: pages 110, 134, 135, 136, 137, 138, and 139; Paulette Johnson: pages viii, 9, 17, 25, 34, 40, 49, 54, 59, 60, 72, 76, 82, 94, 96, 100, 104, 113, 115, 118, 119, 121, 129, 131, and 132; Pets by Paulette: pages v, vii, 2, 3, 4, 5, 6, 7, 14, 18, 23, 24, 27, 28, 33, 37, 39, 42, 43, 47, 48, 61, 63, 71, 79, 80, 81, 84, 87, 90, 93, 98, 103, 107, 117, 126, 144 (top), 145, 149, 152, 155, and 160; Shutterstock: pages iii, 16, 66, 69, and 130

Cover Credits

Shutterstock: front and back cover.

All inquiries should be addressed to:
Barron's Educational Series, Inc.
250 Wireless Boulevard
Hauppauge, New York 11788
www.barronseduc.com

ISBN-10: 0-7641-6231-4 (Book)
ISBN-13: 978-0-7641-6231-2 (Book)
ISBN-10: 0-7641-8678-7 (DVD)
ISBN-13: 978-0-7641-8678-3 (DVD)
ISBN-10: 0-7641-9628-6 (Package)
ISBN-13: 978-0-7641-9628-7 (Package)

Library of Congress Catalog Card No: 2008042209

Library of Congress Cataloging-in-Publication Data
Coile, D. Caroline.
    Dachshunds / D. Caroline Coile.
      p. cm.
    Includes index.
    ISBN-13: 978-0-7641-6231-2
    ISBN-10: 0-7641-6231-4
    ISBN-13: 978-0-7641-8678-3
    ISBN-10: 0-7641-8678-7
    ISBN-13: 978-0-7641-9628-7
    ISBN-10: 0-7641-9628-6
    [etc.]
1. Dachshunds. I. Title.

SF429.D25C637 2009
636.753'8—dc22
                                        2008042209

Printed in China

9 8 7 6 5 4 3 2

CONTENTS

CONTENTS

PREFACE

With one of the most easily recognized silhouettes in the dog world, and one of the most endearing personalities in all the world, the Dachshund has wormed its way into hearts and laps everywhere. Dachshunds are different; that's why we love them. But it's also why Dachshund caretakers need to learn about their special abilities, characteristics, and needs. This book is the ultimate source for all things Dachshund, whether it's fun stuff like their history with royalty or in art and literature, serious stuff like preventing back problems, or practical stuff like convincing them that "come" doesn't mean to run the other way, and "go potty" doesn't mean do it on the floor.

With chapters devoted to history; Dachshund pros and, yes, cons; Dachshund choices, including size, coat type, and color, as well as your best sources for them; puppy care, including Dachshund socialization and early training; Dachshund behavior (and misbehavior); Dachshund-specific health and diet considerations; Dachshund activities and competitions; grooming the three coat types; senior Dachshunds; and why the Dachshund is built like it is, the book will convert you into a Dachshund expert in no time!

Chapter One

All About Dachshunds

S hort on leg but long on life, Dachshunds are one of the most popular
dogs in the world. Rising from a newcomer on the dog scene just a
couple of centuries ago, the Dachshund has taken over by conquering
one heart at a time.

Dawn of the Dachshund

Short-legged dogs have been around at least since ancient Roman times,
when they were used to go underground after small mammals. Such dogs
had to be short and narrow enough to fit in small passageways and burrows, but with sufficient body weight and strength to overpower the burrow's inhabitant. Although it's tempting to point to these dogs as the
Dachshund's ancestors, the truth is that short-legged dogs arise again and
again throughout history, and those of the ancient Romans were more terrier-like than Dachshund-like. In the Dark Ages, other short-legged dogs
with more hound-like features were used to trail game through thick brush
at a pace enabling hunters to follow on foot. Although these may have been
the Dachshund's forebears, there's simply not enough evidence to know.

The First Dachshunds

Only in the 1700s do dogs appear that were definitely Dachshunds. At that
time German foresters began using a French dog called the Bracke to hunt
badgers as well as rabbits, foxes, and wild boar. The Bracke was the proto-
type for the scent hound, with long hanging ears and a desire to pursue and
catch mammals. As some became more specialized for badger hunting, they
were called *dachsbracke* (*dachs* meaning "badger" in German). These dogs
were about 30 to 40 pounds, but such size wasn't needed for hunting
smaller animals, and it was also a hindrance in the confines of a badger
den (or sett).

By the late 1700s, a smaller version called the Dachshund (badger dog)
emerged. These dogs could be as small as 20 pounds; any smaller, and they
couldn't take on a badger. Badger dogs had to be tough and tenacious

FYI: Badger Dogs and Badger Digs

The Eurasian badger, which is the species the Dachshund hunted in Europe, typically weighs from 20 to 35 pounds, and is among the most ferocious of mammals when it comes to defending itself. They live in pairs or in clans of up to a dozen animals in a system of interconnected tunnels and chambers called a sett. These may be simple, with just one or two entrances and chambers, or complex, with dozens of entrances and chambers and hundreds of yards of tunnels. Badgers initially run from dogs, trying to escape into their sett. If they are cornered, they try to tuck their heads between their forelegs and rely on their thick fur and skin for protection. When this occurs, the Dachshund either tries to draw the badger out, or barks at it, dashing in and out at it. If the dog continues, the badger will strike out in self-defense, using powerful jaws and large teeth to inflict damage. If the sett is small, and the badger not too big, the Dachshund may be able to drag it out; more often, the hunters start digging, guided by the Dachshund's barks. In the past ladies would sometimes bring picnic baskets to watch, as the men might spend hours digging. Badger digging was outlawed in the United Kingdom in 1973, and is now illegal in several other European countries.

enough to plunge into a dark sett, traverse downward scenting after their prey, and upon finding it, either tackle it and heft it back up, or more often, hold it at bay while barking until the hunters dug down to them by following the underground racket. Even smaller sizes were used for hunting foxes and rabbits.

Royal Affairs

Dachshunds appealed not only to hunters, but to German nobility, who tended to value good hunting dogs. When Prince Albert (of Saxe-Coburg-Gotha) married Queen Victoria of England in 1839, he introduced Queen Victoria to Dachshunds. Queen Victoria was a great admirer of dogs, and her Dachshunds soon became favorites. Just as celebrities can popularize certain breeds today by being seen in public with them, so did the queen's affection for her Dachshunds cause everyone to want one.

The breed continued to grow in popularity in Germany, but the German Revolution in 1848 disrupted German life, and such luxuries as badger hunting for sport

or the keeping and breeding of pure breeds took a backseat. Some dedicated hunters as well as some wealthier fanciers were able to keep several populations of Dachshunds through the Revolution, however, so that after the Revolution the breed was able to recover. Throughout the 1800s, Germany was known as the center of Dachshund quality.

Dog Shows and Dachshunds

Also in the mid- and late 1800s, the exhibition and judging of dogs became popular. The first dog show was held in England in 1859. By the late 1800s, standards were written for every breed that could be identified, and dogs were judged against these standards with the idea that by selecting those that conformed to the standards for breeding, the breed could

Fun Facts

Dachshund Capital

Gergweis, Germany, is called the Dachshund Capital of the World. In this town, Dachshunds are said to outnumber people two to one, and tourists can rent a Dachshund to take for a walk.

3

be improved. In 1879, a Dachshund named Feldman made history when he became the first Dachshund to prance into a show ring. Although some people still owned Dachshunds mainly for hunting, more often, Dachshunds were being seen parading around a ring with a fancy lady or haughty duke at the end of the leash. The world's first Dachshund club was established in 1881, in England, with members boasting some of society's elite.

Fun Facts

Penthouse View

Despite its country roots, the Dachshund was the most popular breed in Manhattan in 2004.

Dog shows also emerged in Germany, with the first German standard for the Dachshund approved in 1888. In 1895, the first national German club, the Deutsche Teckel Klub, was formed. The Dachshund, or Teckel as it's known in Germany, climbed to become not just one of that country's most successful show dogs, but also a popular pet.

Dachshunds in America

Dachshunds came to America in the mid- to late 1800s. At first hunters used them as they did in Europe, in pursuit of badgers and other small mammals. But they quickly became more known as show dogs and companions than as hunters. The first Dachshund was recognized by the American Kennel Club (AKC) in 1885, and they were exhibited at dog shows even before then. Fanciers formed the Dachshund Club of America in 1895, and by 1913, the breed had one of the largest entries at the Westminster Kennel Club dog show.

In the early 1900s, the Dachshund seemed ready to win over America. Then came World War I. Because Dachshunds were seen as a symbol of Germany, American passions turned against the little dog, to the point that even Dachshund owners and breeders were persecuted. In an attempt to de-Germanize the Dachshund, the AKC changed its name to Badger Dog in 1919, but it had little effect. In 1923, when the AKC changed the name back to Dachshund, only 26 new Dachshunds were registered.

The war decimated the breed as it existed in America, but at the same time, it won the Dachshund new friends. American servicemen returning from Europe had fallen under their spell, and a new influx of Dachshunds arrived in America. Most of these dogs had uncertain backgrounds and couldn't be AKC registered, but they played an even more important role of rewinning the hearts of Americans. It took only a few years before they'd conquered America from within.

World War II did not have the decimating effect on Dachshunds that World War I did,

perhaps because it was already such an American fixture. By 1940, the Dachshund had risen to become the sixth most popular breed in America, and it has continued as one of America's favorite breeds since.

Dachshund Timeline

Early 1400s: Artwork in tombs at Katherine's Church (Oppenheim, Germany) depicts short-legged Dachshund-like dogs.

1561: Perhaps the earliest illustration of earth dogs at work appears in the treatise on hunting *La Venerie*; however, they do not appear to be Dachshunds as we know them.

1582: A woodcut illustrating a badger and rabbit hunt features a dog with a slender body and docked tail, more terrier-like than Dachshund-like.

1671: A little dog for tracking rabbits, and also chasing badgers and foxes, is described in a booklet on hunting and falconry. The dog is said to sometimes have crooked legs, sometimes straight. Some breed historians believe the dog referred to is a Dachshund.

1700: A dog with a long, slender body, and low, somewhat turned-in little legs is described for hunting badgers. The dog is said to come in various colors, but mostly brown, gray, and otter-colored, and sometimes black.

1719: The first illustrations of dogs clearly recognizable as Dachshunds are published in a German hunting book. They are identified as *Tachs Kriecher* and *Tachs Krieger*, and are said to trail and chase game, bark while in pursuit, and point at game. The dogs are said to be most often red or black.

1734: Small, short-legged dogs are mentioned for their ability to hunt in underground passages.

Breed Truths

In English, it's Dachshund. But the Dachshund goes by other names in other languages.

- German: *Deutsche teckel* or *dackel*
- Dutch: *teckel* or *dashond*
- Swedish: *tax*
- Norwegian: *dachshund* for the standards, and *dvergdachshund* and *kanindachshund* for smaller sizes
- Finnish: *mäyräkoira*
- Hungarian: *tacsko*
- Polish: *jamnik*
- Russian: *taksa*
- Italian: *bassotto*

1793: The famous book *Buffon's Natural History* mentions Dachshunds with both straight and crooked legs, and describes them as very snappy and able to chase badgers from their holes. The illustration shows a low-built dog, but with longer legs than today's Dachshunds.

1797: The following description appears: "The Dachshund is of all the hunting dogs the smallest and the weakest, but he surpasses them all in courage. He searches for his far superior enemy deep inside the earth and fights him in his own home territory for endless hours, yes, even for days ..."

1812: Another Dachshund description: "They are snappy, often pugnacious, brave, but often quarrelsome animals, who are tenacious of life. They tend to start fights with any dog, no matter how large he is." The wirehaired Dachshund is also first mentioned.

1820: First mention of the longhaired Dachshund.

1836: First mention of smooth, wirehaired, and longhaired Dachshunds together.

1839: Prince Albert marries Queen Victoria, bringing Dachshunds to England with him.

1840: The first German all-breed studbook is published. It lists 54 Dachshunds.

1841: A painting of Waldman, one of Queen Victoria's Dachshunds, shows a black and tan dog with white chest and crooked legs.

1848: The German Revolution places dog breeding and badger hunting low on the list of priorities in Germany.

1859: The first recorded dog show is held, in England.

1866: The first Dachshunds compete at English dog shows. They compete in the class for foreign sporting dogs, and are called German Badger Hounds.

1870: The first recorded Dachshunds arrive in America.

1873: The Crystal Palace dog show in England is the first to grant Dachshunds separate breed status.

1877: A smooth Dachshund is shown at the Westminster Kennel Club, the first Dachshund entered at that prestigious show.

1879: The first German Dachshund standard is written. Also, the first Dachshund, a dog name Feldman, enters the show ring.

1881: The English Dachshund Club is formed.

1884: The American Kennel Club (AKC) is formed.

1885: The AKC registers its first Dachshund, named Dash.

1888: The German Dachshund Club (Deutsche Teckel Klub) is formed, and the first German standard is approved.

1890: The AKC officially recognizes the wirehaired variety.

1895: The Dachshund Club of America is formed.

1914: World War I breaks out. Dachshunds become unpopular in America because of their association with Germany.

1919: The AKC changes the breed's name to Badger Dog in an attempt to distance it from Germany.

1923: In America, the breed's name is changed back to Dachshund. Only 26 Dachshunds are registered that year. In England, a longhaired Dachshund named Ratzmann von Habichtscof puts longhairs on the map by winning Best in Show at Crufts, the world's largest dog show at the time.

1924: The AKC divides breeds into groups, placing the Dachshund in the Working group.

1929: The Dachshund is transferred to the Sporting group.

1930: Dachshunds are ranked 28th in AKC popularity.

1931: The Dachshund is switched to the newly formed Hound group. Also in that year, the first longhair is registered with the AKC.

1934: First separate classes for miniature Dachshunds are offered.

1935: American field trials for Dachshunds are organized.

1940: Dachshunds are ranked sixth in AKC popularity. They have remained among America's most popular breeds since.

1943: For the first time, each of the three coat varieties advances to group competitions in AKC shows, rather than just one variety.

1948: An influx of high-quality miniatures comes to America from Europe. Two years later the movie *Fancy Pants* introduces the American public to miniatures.

1952: The National Miniature Dachshund Club is formed in the United States. It continues today.

1972: The Dachshund is chosen as the official mascot for the 1972 Summer Olympics in Germany. The mascot is named Waldi.

Fun Facts

Waldi

What better mascot for the 1972 Summer Olympics in Germany than a Dachshund? The logo of "Waldi" was a longhaired Dachshund modeled after a real Dachshund named Cherie von Birkenhof. They chose a Dachshund as mascot not only because it was German, but because it represented the attributes needed by Olympic athletes: resistance, tenacity, and agility.

Dachshunds in Art

Although short-legged hunting dogs were often depicted in art since at least the 1400s, the first Dachshund-like dogs don't appear in art until the early 1700s. Even so, these dogs are not necessarily Dachshunds, since even in 1793 they are identified simply as Bassets (a generic French term used to describe short-legged dogs).

Only after 1840, when Queen Victoria received her first Dachshund, Waldman, does the Dachshund begin to be the main subject of beautifully executed paintings. The queen commissioned the best animal artists of her day to paint her favorite pets. An 1841 painting of Waldman by George Morley shows a dog that would be easily recognizable as a Dachshund today, although he would certainly not be a show winner. His front legs were bowed to the point of looking deformed. The Dachshund portraits remain in the royal collection.

By 1870, Dachshund portraits looked more like today's dogs, with straighter front legs. They also tended to be depicted with more mischievous expressions! Some of the best nineteenth-century Dachshund art was painted by Arthur Wardle, Maud Earl, Edwin Landseer, and John Sargent Noble. The dogs are almost always smooths, either red or black and tan. An 1888 painting by William Henry Hamilton Trood, however, clearly shows a merle Dachshund.

In the 1900s, Dachshund depictions became more whimsical, and by the mid-1900s the Dachshund had become one of the most popular breeds for fun art and canine knickknacks.

Certainly the best-known work of Dachshund art is Giacomo Balla's *Dynamism of a Dog on a Leash* (1912), considered by some as one of the 100 most important artworks of the twentieth century. Balla considered it a primary objective of the Futurism movement, of which he was a proponent, to depict movement, and he could scarcely have chosen a better model than a dynamic Dachshund!

Pierre Bonnard included a Dachshund in the foreground of his well-known impressionist piece *Nude in a Bath* (1946), as well as many others. His own Dachshund was his constant companion.

Pablo Picasso often included his own Dachshund, Lump (German for "rascal") in his works—although not always recognizably! Lump slept with Picasso and ate at the table off his own plate. There's even a book about them: *Picasso & Lump: A Dachshund's Odyssey*. Picasso said of Lump: "Lump is not a dog, not a man—he really is someone else."

Andy Warhol was also influenced by his Dachshund. A longtime cat lover, Warhol was given a Dachshund puppy in the 1970s, which he took everywhere with him—to his studio, interviews, art openings, and gala affairs. During interviews, he would often direct questions to the dog, Archie. Archie was eventually joined by another Dachshund, Amos. Warhol began doing pet portraits, often aided by Archie and Amos as models. His *Portrait of Maurice*, which hangs in the Gallery of Modern Art, was a commissioned portrait of a friend's Dachshund.

David Hockney is among the current well-known artists influenced by his Dachshunds, Stanley and Boodgie, whom he describes as "intelligent, loving, comical, and often bored." As models, he admits, they are not very good. "One knock on the door is enough to make them leap up." Nonetheless, he published a book of his Dachshund portraits, mostly of them sleeping or horizontal, called *Dog Days*.

Cartoonist **Gary Larson** favors Dachshunds for his canine models, and even produced a book called *Weiner Dog Art*, which features Dachshunds in various famous works of art.

Dachshunds in Literature

Not only can you not help but smile when you see a Dachshund, but you can't help but feel good when you read about them. Maybe that's why Dachshunds are the stars of so many children's books. H. A. and Margret Ray included their Dachshunds' antics in their *Curious George* and *Pretzel* books. It's not just kids' books, though; several Dachshund books that target children have just as much appeal for adults.

Wirehaired Dachshund Howie Monroe is the star of a series of children's books, *Tales from the House of Bunnicula* (by James Howe), in which Howie tries his paw at becoming a writer in various genres, always with comedic results.

The House of Tekeldon, by Denys Dawnay, is a jaunt through history of one Dachshund family's comically fictitious adventures through the centuries.

Nor is the compulsion to write about Dachshunds new. The nineteenth-century British poet Matthew Arnold, who owned several Dachshunds, eulogized his dog Geist in one of the most quoted canine eulogies, "Geist's Grave."

Most passages mentioning Dachshunds are done in true Dachshund spirit, with a sense of biting humor. Mark Twain, upon seeing a dog that obviously matched the description of a Dachshund, remarked on the dog's poor design, saying he was built like a bad bench. Of his conversation with the dog's owner in *Following the Equator*, he reported: "He said that when he walked along in London, people often stopped and looked at the dog. Of course I did not say anything, for I did not want to hurt his feelings, but I could have explained to him that if you take a great long low dog like that and waddle it along the street anywhere in the world and not charge anything, people will stop and look." Not content to let the matter of the Dachshund drop, Twain again poked fun in an article about his attempt to become an artist, called "Instructions in Art," in which he sketched the back half of a Dachshund. He said of the sketch: "The next picture is part of an animal, but I do not know the name of it. It is not finished. The front end of it went around a corner before I could get to it."

Fun Facts

Three Dachshund films of special note:

- *Dicky's Demon Dachshund*, a short silent movie made in 1915, may be the earliest film featuring the Dachshund. The title says it all!
- *Fancy Pants*, starring Bob Hope and Lucille Ball, was released in 1950. It's important in Dachshund history because it brought the miniature Dachshund to the attention of the public for the first time.
- *The Ugly Dachshund*, released in 1966, stars a Dachshund dam and her wrecking-crew puppies (along with a Great Dane puppy who thinks he's a Dachshund). The movie was adapted from a 1938 novel of the same name.

Prolific author P. G. Wodehouse is best known for his stories about a bachelor and his articulate and resourceful valet named Jeeves. Some have gone so far as to speculate that Jeeves was modeled after Wodehouse's Dachshund, Bertie. In an obviously Dachshund-inspired moment, Wodehouse once wrote: "It is fatal to let any dog know that he is funny, for he immediately loses his head and starts hamming it up." Wodehouse was apt to use his experiences with Dachshunds to conjure up a clever comparison, as in this passage from *Service With a Smile:* "Her brow was furrowed, her lips drawn, and the large brown eyes which rested on George Cyril Wellbeloved had in them something of the sadness one sees in those of a Dachshund which, coming to the dinner table to get its ten per cent, is refused a cut off the joint."

Dachshunds in Film

Dachshunds appear in many film and television productions, but working with a Dachshund is always an adventure. Not only are they prone to ad lib, such as when the Dachshund in *The Bonfire of the Vanities* decided it would be a nice touch to throw up on costar Kirsten Dunst, but they have a bad habit of stealing the scene.

Animated Dachshunds, being easier to work with, and far less demanding, appear more often in starring roles. In the early Mickey Mouse cartoons, Mickey's sidekick was a Dachshund. And in later Disney animated films featuring Pluto, Dinah the Dachshund was Pluto's love interest.

Dachshunds and celebrities have a long-running relationship, withstanding the whims of fad breeds to span more than a century of star power. Maybe it's not that celebrities make their Dachshunds into stars, but that Dachshunds make their people into celebrities!

Dachshunds at Court

Despite their humble beginnings as hunting dogs, it wasn't long before Dachshunds burrowed into the laps, and hearts, of people in every walk of life. With their expectation of royal treatment, Dachshunds have been special favorites with the aristocracy.

Queen Victoria had many breeds of dogs, but Dachshunds were an early favorite. One of the first Dachshunds in England was Waldman, sent from Germany in 1840, followed by Deckel in 1845. Deckel impressed the queen when he pounced on a rat at Windsor. The queen remarked, "The rat made an awful noise, though he was killed right out pretty quickly." Deckel was the origin of five generations of Windsor Dachshunds, although in later generations the queen never bred from the dogs she chose as personal pets. It was her association with the breed that launched the Dachshund into social prominence in London in the late 1800s.

Grand Duke Alexander was an unwilling Dachshund owner. He once complained of strict childhood regulations that limited their choice of household pets to German Dachshunds and Persian cats.

Hapsburg Crown Prince Rudolph left his Dachshunds to "poor huntsmen" in his will.

Kaiser William II owned about a dozen Dachshunds at a time, and was said to be closer to them than to all his faithful servants. The dogs had few admirers outside of the kaiser, as they were described as "biting, snarling

little brutes with jaws measuring half the length of their smooth bodies, and a corresponding penchant for people's calves, skirts, and petticoats… These pets follow his Majesty everywhere, and when they make inroads on folks' flesh and blood, or clothes, William, who protects and coddles them, thinks it huge fun." The dogs regularly demolished fine furnishings and ran amok. Two of his Dachshunds, Wadl and Hexl, almost caused an international incident when they visited the Austro-Hungarian crown prince's estate and immediately dispatched a priceless golden pheasant (Palatine Princess: Letters of Madame, Duchess of Orleans. Translated by G. S. Stevenson, London, 1924, 2.85–6). During World War I and the kaiser's subsequent exile, his dog Senta remained by his side. Senta died at age 20 and is buried near William's grave.

Princess Aspasia of Greece (1896–1972), wife of King Alexander, was never without a longhaired Dachshund. When entering England in 1941, she was caught trying to smuggle her Dachshund, Tulip, under her coat to avoid quarantine. She wept uncontrollably when the dog was taken from her.

Queen Elizabeth II and Princess Margaret shared a love of long and low dogs. Princess Margaret was a long-time Dachshund lover, but her dogs were perhaps best known for their indiscretions, such as the tryst her male Dachshund, Pipkin, had with Queen Elizabeth's female Corgi. The resulting "dorgis" became favorites of the queen.

Ten Famous Dachshunds

Every Dachshund is famous in his own mind, but only a few achieve fame that lasts through the years or reaches around the world. Whether they earned their fame through show-ring wins or extraordinary feats, following are some of the Dachshund greats.

1. **Champion Jackdaw, Setting the Standard:** During his long show career in England, Jackdaw, a black and tan standard smooth born in 1886, was never once defeated. The Jackdaw Trophy is offered to this day for the top winning Dachshund of all types in England each year.
2. **Champion Kensal Call Boy, American First:** A black and tan standard smooth born in 1927, Call Boy became the first Dachshund to win an AKC Best in Show.
3. **Champion Herman Rinkton, Ring Master:** A red standard smooth, Herman was the first American Dachshund to become a big winner. Exhibited in the late 1930s, he won 14 Best in Show awards.
4. **Champion Favorite von Marienlust, Changing the Breed:** Born in the 1940s, he became one of the most influential producers the breed has known, setting much of the type we see today. Not only does he hold the record as the top producing sire of champions, with 95 to his credit, but his sons hold the number two and number three spots, with 90 and 82 champions, respectively.

5. Crackerjack, Westminster Wonder: The Westminster Kennel
Club is America's most prestigious dog show, and its second-oldest
sporting event. Yet in all the years that Dachshunds have been
competing there, only five times has one won the Hound group.
Ch. Crosswynd's Crackerjack, a smooth standard, managed that feat
not just once, but twice, in 1968 and 1969. Other Dachshund winners
of the Hound group at Westminster are the smooth Ch Foc vom
Teckelhof (1938), the smooth Ch White Gables Ristocrat (1961),
the longhaired Ch Pramada's Curmudgeon L, and the wirehaired
Ch Starbarrack Malachite SW.

6. **Gretl, Long on Brains:** The top obedience award offered by the American Kennel Club is the Obedience Trial Champion title, or OTCH. The title requires dogs to follow hand signals, distinguish among scent articles, and heel, sit, jump, stay, and come with almost perfect scores. Gretl was not only the first Dachshund, but the first hound, to earn an OTCH. Gretl (her official name is OTCH Mayrhofen Olympischer Star L) also won Top Dog at the 1978 Obedience World Series.

7. **Brutus, Low Dog in High Places:** Brutus is the world record holder of 15,000 feet for the highest skydiving dog. Apparently born with a need for adrenaline rushes, Brutus started going up in the air with his owner when the dog would chase his owner's plane down the runway. Once up, the safest thing to do was to take Brutus along on the way down, and the dog loved it. Of course, he dives in tandem with his owner, not be trusted to pull the cord on time. Brutus has appeared on about 30 television programs.

8. **Baron, Dragstrip Dachshund:** Not everyone approves of Dachshund racing, but nobody can deny that Baron (officially, CarrDox's Bear Mountain Baron) dominated the sport when he was finally asked to retire in 2000 after four years (and two *Tonight Show* appearances) so that other Dachshunds could have a chance. Baron wasn't only undefeated; he never even had any close calls. His record of 50 yards in 4.22 seconds far bests that of the fastest human sprinter.

9. **Schmaltz, Skiing Sausage Dog:** Schmaltz, a long-haired Dachshund, learned to ski on four little skis, winning fame in the 1970s throughout the United States, Canada, and Europe. He appeared in skiing movies and on many television shows and was the subject of a book on skiing safety, *"Track Right With Schmaltz."*

10. **Your Dachshund!**

10 Questions About Dachshund History

1 **Did the Egyptian pharaohs have Dachshunds?** You'll sometimes read that Dachshunds date back to the times of the ancient Egyptians. That's a fallacy that probably arose from a carving of a dog along with a hieroglyphic inscription that was erroneously interpreted as reading *tekal* or *tekar* on a monument of Thutmose III. The Dachshund is known as the *teckel* in Germany, and as such, some people thought the somewhat short-legged dog in the carving must be a Dachshund. It wasn't. The hieroglyphs actually spelled out *tqru* and further, the German word *teckel* can be traced back to Germanic roots.

2 **Is the Dachshund really a hound?** The AKC places the Dachshund in its Hound group, although it wasn't always there. During much of the 1920s, it was in the AKC Working group. Then it spent two years in the Sporting group before finally settling into the Hound group in 1931. The Dachshund's designation as a hound probably originated as a failure to communicate. When Dachshunds were first becoming popular in England, the *hund* of Dachshund was misinterpreted as meaning "hound" rather than its true German meaning of "dog." True, Dachshunds can be used like hounds to trail rabbits and other mammals, but the Dachshund's forte is as an earthdog, which is the terrier's domain.

3 **What causes the Dachshund's short legs?** Most short-legged dogs have a condition called *achondroplasia* in which the leg bones stop growing in length but continue to grow in diameter. Dachshunds share the same type of growth plates seen in achondroplastic dwarfs, but they do not share the same genes. Instead, their condition may be caused by chondroplasia, which causes changes in growth plates throughout the body.

4 **Why do Dachshunds come in different coat types?** It's no accident that Dachshunds come in different sizes and coat types. The smooth coat was good for use in most areas and temperate weather. But in cold weather, the long coat afforded more warmth. Unfortunately, the long coat tended to get weighted down with mud and brambles when working in wet areas or thickets. The wire coat gave the dog the best protection against brambles without getting bogged down.

5 **Why do Dachshunds come in different sizes?** The earliest Dachshunds weighed more than 30 pounds, and descended from larger dogs that were used to hunt a variety of mammals, including wild boar, badger, fox, and wounded deer. Smaller dogs, around 15 to 20 pounds, were better for pursuing fox and deer because they could squeeze through thickets. Even smaller Dachshunds, weighing less than ten pounds, were ideal for hunting rabbits.

Which hot dog came first, the weiner or the Dachshund? In 1852, frankfurters were born in Frankfurt, Germany, with the better known made by a butcher known for his Dachshund. His frankfurters became known as Dachshund sausages. Around 1895, sausage vendors sold Dachshund sausages outside student dormitories, and their carts became known as dog carts. The first recorded use of the term *hot dog* occurs in an 1895 *Yale Record,* although the name didn't catch on until 1902, when vendors hawking Dachshund sausages at a cold Giants baseball game urged patrons to get their "Dachshund sausages while they're red hot!" A sports cartoonist, Tad Dorgan, was nearing deadline and quickly drew a cartoon of a frankfurter with a tail, legs, and head so it looked like a Dachshund. Not knowing how to spell the name, he captioned it "hot dog!" The name stuck. The frankfurter may have gotten its hot dog nickname from the Dachshund, but the Dachshund got its weiner dog nickname from the frankfurter.

Did Plato, Cleopatra, Napoleon, Michelangelo, Leonardo, Rubens, Shakespeare, and General Patton own Dachshunds? They didn't own Dachshunds because in most cases, Dachshunds weren't around. The Internet reports are the product of the fertile imagination of a Dachshund web site creator who made up stories to present a fanciful history of the Dachshund that mixes truth and fiction. The site clearly labels its content as such, but most people didn't read the disclaimer, and went on to copy the information on their sites.

Just how popular are Dachshunds? In Germany, Dachshunds have remained one of the most popular breeds for more than a century. They experienced a boost in numbers after the 1972 Olympics in Germany, where a Dachshund was the mascot. But in the last decade or so, their numbers have fallen by about 40 percent.

In the United States, after the popularity plummet during World War I, Dachshunds advanced steadily. From 1930 to 1940, they rose from 28th to 6th in AKC registrations. They've remained among America's top dogs since then, ranking seventh in popularity in 2007.

How many countries are Dachshunds found in? Dachshunds are found in almost every, if not every, country in the world. They are especially popular in all European countries, North America, Japan, Australia, New Zealand, Russia, South Africa, and Central and South America. They are found on every continent but Antarctica.

How has the Dachshund changed in the last century? Dachshunds are generally more gregarious and easygoing now, because they've been bred more for companionship than hunting. They're also longer and lower, with deeper chest and more prominent keel (forechest). The miniature size has become more popular with pet owners than the standard size, and there's greater variety in coat type and color.

19

Chapter Two

The Mind of the Dachshund

Whether rooting after a backyard mole or snorting after that treat he buried in your sofa cushions, all Dachshunds have one thing in common: they'll burrow their way deep into your heart, dig their heels in, and never let go.

The World According to Dachshunds

Some dogs will wait, breathless, for your next command, complete only if they're doing your bidding. Tell that to a Dachshund, and he'll roll around laughing. Do your bidding? No, it's the other way around, at least in his mind. Fear not, though, he's a generous master, never stingy with the rewards he'll dole out in tail wags and wet kisses.

The Dachshund's world is full of beckoning adventure, whether it takes him to fight dust badgers under the bed, challenge that dog next door, or search the fence yet again for weak spots that spell escape. Because even better than the adventures the home and yard hold are the forbidden ones on the other side of the fence.

It's not that Dachshunds are willfully disobedient. Well, maybe just a little. But they can't help it. The Dachshund's DNA is true to what its ancestors were bred to do: hunt tough quarry on their own. As a hunter, the Dachshund must

- follow his nose. The Dachshund is always on the lookout for new scents, wandering abroad in search of trails to follow and holes to investigate.
- not be swayed from his mission once on the trail—even when you're chasing after and calling him.
- be self-directed, making his own decisions. A hunting dog that had to check back with a person would end up with quarry that simply sauntered away when the dog's attention was diverted. That means he won't ask you what to do—he'll simply assume he knows the answer.
- be tough and tenacious. A dog that needs to face off against a badger underground needs to persevere in the face of adversity. That means

he won't be easily discouraged by your stern looks and admonitions. You've got nothing on an angry badger!

- be an enthusiastic barker. To dig down to where the Dachshund was holding the badger at bay, the dog needed to bark, loudly and consistently, for a long time. Otherwise the hunters would be digging at random, and might even collapse the sett or hit the dog.
- squeeze into tight places, including through tiny gaps in the fence you never thought a dog could fit through.
- be a problem solver. If you repair that gap in the fence, your Dachshund will consider it a personal challenge to find another route.

So that's the Dachshund: adventurous, resourceful, and very much his own dog. He may seem mischievous and hard headed, and in a way he is, but he's really acting like he was bred to act—just doing so in your home, not the forests of Germany.

But that's only half the Dachshund. Yes, he's a hunter at heart. But he's also a lover. He adores draping his long body

Breed Truths

Dachshund Personality

- Bold
- Independent
- Clever
- Adventurous
- Energetic
- Watchful
- Tenacious
- Loving

COMPATIBILITY Is a Dachshund the Best Breed for You?

	Rating
ENERGY LEVEL	● ● ●
EXERCISE REQUIREMENTS	● ●
PLAYFULNESS	● ● ●
AFFECTION LEVEL	● ● ●
FRIENDLINESS TOWARD OTHER PETS	● ●
FRIENDLINESS TOWARD STRANGERS	●
FRIENDLINESS TOWARD CHILDREN	● ● ●
EASE OF TRAINING	● ●
GROOMING REQUIREMENTS	
SMOOTH	●
LONG	● ●
WIRE	● ● ●
SHEDDING	
SMOOTH	● ● ●
LONG	● ● ●
WIRE	●
SPACE REQUIREMENTS	● ●
OK FOR BEGINNERS	● ● ● ●

4 Dots = Highest rating on scale

over your lap and snoozing away the evening. He'll squirm over on his back and wriggle around, his way of asking for a belly rub. He'll cock his head at your questions and offer a paw when times are tough. He'll wag his tail with whiplike speed at the prospect of sharing a game or a walk or a ride in the car. He'll follow you from room to room, and poke his nose into whatever you're working on. If you have a fun idea, he's game! But come nighttime, he's equally adept at snuggling close and sharing your bed.

He'll make you laugh, at times he'll make you grumble, but as long as he's by your side, he'll make you happy.

Dachshund Pros and Cons

Dachshunds have a lot going for them. They must, to be one of the most popular breeds around, and to keep that position for so long. Perhaps the question isn't why they're so popular, but why anyone would choose any other dog?

But like any dog, the Dachshund isn't for everyone.

- If you want a dog to hop to your every command, that's not a Dachshund. Most are very bright and quick to learn, but they're also independent and don't appreciate being bossed around. If you train your dog using rewards, rather than force, you're more likely to get a Dachshund who will mind you (unless something else more interesting is going on) rather than battle you. Dachshunds have achieved high honors in obedience, but they're not like retrievers and herding dogs that were bred to work following human direction.

- If you want a dog to lie quietly at your feet all day, that's not a Dachshund. Dachshunds are small but energetic. They have to exercise their bodies and minds every day. Fortunately, their needs are not great; a walk around the neighborhood, or a vigorous game session in the backyard, are really all it takes to drain off excessive energy. A short training session will help further tire him. Dachshunds can also get a fair amount of exercise just running back and forth inside. Given adequate exercise, though, your Dachshund will lie quietly, not at your feet, but at your side, where he is sure he belongs.

- If you want a dog to be your jogging companion, that's not a Dachshund. That is, unless you just want to jog around the block. It's true that Dachshunds can run farther than you'd think, but those short legs have limits, so if you really want a jogging partner, choose something with longer legs.

- If you want a dog to play fetch with, that's not a Dachshund. Yes, Dachshunds enjoy a good game of fetch when they're in the mood. But unlike retrievers and many other breeds, they're not always in the mood.

- If you want a dog who loves everybody, that's not a Dachshund. Dachshunds tend to be wary of strangers, warming up only after they've gotten to know them. The upside is that the Dachshund is a loyal dog, decidedly devoted to one family.

Dachshunds with Kids and with Other Pets

Kids

Bring a Dachshund into your household, and it's like adding another kid. Kids and Dachshunds share that same sense of fun and adventure, but don't be surprised if they also share a talent for mischief.

A child and a Dachshund can form a friendship that will last well into your child's teens, and one that may be as close as that of siblings. Don't be surprised if your Dachshund consistently chooses your child's bed over yours, or prefers her company. Kids are fun!

In general, children and Dachshunds make a good pair. But they're not the ideal match, for a few reasons:

- Dachshunds aren't really built for rough-and-tumble play, especially if they're picked up and dropped, or encouraged to twist and jump. Such activities can bring on back problems in Dachshunds already predisposed, and unfortunately, a lot of Dachshunds are predisposed. Teach children to play with the dog on the floor, and caution them against lifting the dog or shoving it. Responsible, gentle children should be fine with a Dachshund, but toddlers may not understand that you cannot push on the dog's back or worse, ride it like a tiny pony.
- Dachshunds have their limits. Some dogs will lie there while their ears are pulled and eyes are poked, but the typical Dachshund will first try to leave, and if that fails, warn off the pestering child. Some parents see this warning growl and discipline the dog, when it's the child who was the instigator. And some Dachshunds, having exhausted every other avenue, may finally snap in self-defense. Parents hold the key to educating and controlling their children. As with any dog, they must monitor dogs and children when they're together, and they must be fair to each. The dog should always have an escape route or an off-limits zone where only he is allowed and children are not allowed.
- Dachshunds won't necessarily stick around. Dachshunds are pretty good at hanging out in the front yard, playing with the kids, but they

are easily enticed away, which can in turn lure away the child. The solution is easy: Don't let them play in an unfenced area. Young children should never be given the responsibility of walking the dog. It's too easy for the dog to get away, or for another dog to attack, and children aren't capable of handling emergencies. Not only could the Dachshund be hurt, but children may be inclined to do heroic, but foolish, things to save their dog.

- Dachshunds may not love your children's friends. As one-family dogs, Dachshunds are often not terribly pleased at strange, rambunctious kids invading their homes. They may not be particularly welcoming. Again, adults should always supervise dogs and children, and the dog should have an area he can escape to or be confined to. By setting up introductions, in which the visiting child gives the dog a treat, or has him do a simple obedience exercise, the Dachshund may be more inclined to welcome visitors.
- A 2008 survey found that Dachshunds were responsible for more dog bites than any other of the 33 breeds in the study.

Other Pets

Dachshunds were bred to hunt badgers, boars, foxes, and rabbits. Before you breathe a sigh of relief that you don't happen to have a pet badger or boar, think what that means in the wider sense. Dachshunds are hunters, through and through. They thrive on tracking down and going after small (and sometimes large) furry animals.

Rodents If you have a Noah's Ark of small rodents wandering around your house, don't think you can turn a Dachshund loose amongst them—not unless you enjoy watching graphic hunt scenes. You can have a pet rabbit, rat, gerbil, or hamster, but you have to make the effort to protect them, especially when you're not there to referee.

This doesn't mean your Dachshund is a bloodthirsty savage

CAUTION

3 Reasons NOT to Buy Your Child a Dachshund

1. Don't buy a Dachshund as a desperate last-minute Christmas gift. Dogs are not impulse items. A puppy shouldn't have to compete with all the distractions during the holidays. If, however, the entire family is sold on the idea, you can have a leash, bowl, or video of your puppy-to-come under the tree.

2. Don't buy a Dachshund as a way to teach a child responsibility. Children seldom live up to their promises of feeding, cleaning up after, grooming, and walking the dog. It's unfair to let the dog suffer in order to teach the child a lesson. In almost every family, Mom ends up taking care of the dog.

3. Don't buy a Dachshund because your child decided one day he wanted one. This is a decision for the entire family, and especially the person who will be in charge of caring for the dog. A week from now the child may not even remember the dog he absolutely had to have or the world would end.

wreaking carnage wherever he goes. But you do have to respect what he was bred to do for hundreds of years. In fact, you can teach your Dachshund to coexist with any of these species, but you still need to be careful. Your best bet for success will come with introducing the dog when he's a puppy. Keep in mind that if a small animal runs, the dog is more likely to chase because it triggers his prey-drive. And Dachshunds have lots of prey-drive. Regardless, never leave your Dachshund and rabbit or rodent together unsupervised.

Cats Prey-drive aside, Dachshunds and cats can not only coexist in peace, but can become fast friends. But a good friendship starts with careful introductions. Keep the dog crated and let the cat wander around, or crate them both near each other until they get used to the other's presence. Then introduce them somewhere the cat can jump up high, or hold the dog on leash. For Dachshund puppies, the greater danger is in the cat swatting the dog in the face rather than the dog hurting the cat. You want to avoid unfriendly overtures, and especially avoid any chasing. Feed the two around each other, so they're more interested in treats, but don't let them steal one another's food. Many Dachshunds and cats have become lifelong friends.

Dogs Hounds as a lot are considered the amiable souls of the dog world. But recall that Dachshunds aren't your typical hounds. Some would characterize them as the terriers of the hound group. Remember, much of the way they hunt is terrier-like. The wires, especially, probably have some terrier ancestry.

Dachshunds tend to be clannish. They are good with other dogs in their own family, and not so good with strange dogs. Multiple-Dachshund families usually work out well, with the Dachshunds becoming inseparable pals. They'll entertain not only each other, but their owners with their

27

never-ending antics. If you have limited home time, or can't play with your dog as much as you'd like, consider adding another dog as a built-in buddy.

That doesn't mean things will always go smoothly. Like all dogs, some Dachshunds can become mortal enemies, itching to fight at the slightest provocation. This is more likely to happen between dogs of the same sex.

Of course, other untoward things are likely to happen between dogs of opposite sexes unless you have them neutered and spayed.

Introduce a new puppy much as you would a dog and a cat, with the puppy in a crate so the older dog can check him out. If the puppy can walk on a leash, taking the two together on short walks is an ideal way to introduce them on neutral ground and have the older dog associate the younger with good times. The older dog has earned seniority, and should never give up rightful place as first dog. That means the puppy doesn't get the older dog's bed or toys or time with you, and doesn't get to pester him. If the puppy does persist in pestering, don't blame the older dog for

BE PREPARED! Are You Ready for a Dachshund?

Before you get a Dachshund, make sure you're ready for a dog in general and a Dachshund in particular.

1. Do you plan to keep this dog his entire life, anticipated to be 10 to 15 years?

2. Is your future settled enough that you won't find yourself having to move to a place that doesn't accept dogs?

3. Does everyone in the family want a dog? This is especially vital if the dog is going to interfere with the family's vacation plans or other activities.

4. Who will care for the dog? This person must really want a dog, not just be agreeing without thinking it through. This person must be an adult.

5. How old are your children? Experts recommend waiting until your children are at least six years old before bringing in a puppy.

6. Is anybody in the house allergic to dogs? Before you get a dog, spend some time around other households with dogs, especially Dachshunds, to make sure nobody is allergic, or that allergies are not too uncomfortable.

7. Where will the dog live? Dogs make better family members and companions when they live with the family in the home. Dogs are social animals and will be very unhappy if forced to live by themselves.

8. Are you home enough to care for a dog? You don't have to be a stay-at-home doggy parent, but if your dog is going to be alone for 12-hour stretches, you're not in a position to have a dog.

9. Do you have a fenced yard? A secure yard makes caring for a dog a lot easier, because you won't always have to walk him at inopportune times.

10. Do you plan to train your dog? Not only does training teach your dog manners that make him easier to live with, but the act of training, when done properly, reinforces bonding.

11. Are you somebody who cannot tolerate mess or some damage to your belongings? Then don't get a dog. No matter how careful you are, something will get chewed up or wet on.

12. Does barking drive you crazy? Dachshunds bark. You can train them to bark less, but barking is part of their nature, and training them to stop will not be easy.

13. Do you expect strict obedience? Then don't get a Dachshund.

14. Do you want a dog that gazes at you adoringly all day long? Better keep some treats in your pocket, then, or get a different breed.

15. Do you want a dog that will bring a smile to your face no matter your mood? Get a Dachshund!

warning him with a growl or gentle snap; somebody has to teach him manners, and if you won't do it, your other dog will! The puppy may shriek and
act as though he's been terrorized, but chances are he's simply scared and
has learned a valuable lesson. The older dog should not be allowed to bully
the puppy, though, or persist in attacks.

Dachshund Health

Few dogs of the Dachshund's short stature are expected to perform as
athletically as is this badger-fighting, rabbit-finding, deer-trailing hunter.
Historically, a Dachshund that couldn't perform at least one of these func-
tions didn't get fed for long. As a result, the Dachshund comes from healthy,
vigorous stock.

But times have changed since the days when the Dachshund was valued
mostly for its hunting prowess. The original Dachshund was slightly longer
in leg and shorter in back, and although we have no records, many suppose
those original dogs had fewer back problems. In fact, the original Dachshund,
which was not as stringently bred within a closed population, may have
had some health advantages. But that is mere conjecture at this point, and
today's better health care has helped circumvent many canine health problems in general.

Like every breed of dog, the Dachshund breed has a closed gene pool,
which means Dachshunds are bred only to Dachshunds to make purebred

Dachshunds. This limited pool of genes increases the possibility that dogs possessing the same possibly recessive genes for a particular hereditary disease will breed with one another. Offspring with copies of the deleterious gene from both parents can be affected by that health disorder. The less related two dogs are, the lower this possibility, which is why when you select a litter, you should look at the pedigree and avoid highly inbred ones (ones in which the sire and dam are related).

Adult Problems

Without doubt, back problems are the Dachshund's number one breed-related health concern (see pages 106–107). About one-quarter of all Dachshunds will develop some degree of disk disease during their life, and some will become paralyzed from the disorder. Back problems are related not so much to the Dachshund's long back as to his short legs. The Dachshund has a type of dwarfism that appears to be related to problems with the cushioning disks between the vertebra.

Aside from back problems, adult Dachshunds have very few breed-related health problems. They are susceptible to obesity, a particularly bad combination for a back susceptible to problems, but you have the power to prevent this simply by controlling what goes into your Dachshund's bowl and stomach.

Puppy Problems

Dachshund puppies are slightly more likely, compared to other breeds, to have retained baby teeth, which must sometimes be removed by a veterinarian so they don't cause problems with the permanent teeth. Dachshunds

are also slightly more likely to have pattern baldness, which is evident in puppyhood. This symmetrical hair loss on both sides of the body doesn't cause any health problems, but can be frustrating for cosmetic reasons.

Senior Problems

As seniors, Dachshunds are much more likely to develop Cushing's syndrome compared to other breeds. In this disease, the adrenal glands produce too much cortisol, causing a variety of symptoms (see page 153). Affected dogs must be treated with medication or they will eventually succumb to the disease.

Health and Choices

Dachshunds are also slightly more prone to many less common disorders (see page 101), but none of these is common enough to be a consideration when choosing the Dachshund as your companion. In fact, the only Dachshund disorder that should warrant consideration is the problem with the back. Any prospective Dachshund owner should consider what they would do if their dog became debilitated because of back problems.

As far as is known, no differences exist in health and longevity between coat varieties or sizes. The only relationship with color and health is that double dapples (see page 40) may have visual or hearing problems.

Longevity

Dachshunds are fairly long-lived, typically living between 12 and 14 years. It is not uncommon, however, to encounter a Dachshund well into its mid- or even late teens.

BE PREPARED! What Will a Dachshund Cost?

- ✔ Puppy: $250–$1,500 ($50–$250 for a shelter or rescue dog).
- ✔ Food: $15–$30 (and up) per month.
- ✔ License: $0–$60 per year.
- ✔ Accessories: $20–$100 per year.
- ✔ Boarding: $15–$30 per day.
- ✔ Obedience classes: $50–$100 per eight-week session.

Veterinary:
- ✔ First year (puppy vaccinations, neuter/spay): $400–$800.
- ✔ Routine years (boosters, checkups, parasite control): $100–$300.
- ✔ Senior years: $200–$500 (assuming no problems; otherwise much higher).
- ✔ Add for each typical illness or accident: $100–$600 (and up).
- ✔ Add for disk disease surgery: $2,000–$4,000.

Note: Costs in metropolitan areas tend to be higher than costs in rural areas.

Are You Ready for a Dachshund?

When you consider adding a Dachshund to your life, do so only with the intention of getting him for keeps. A dog isn't a trial-run item, or a passing interest, but a sentient being who won't understand why he's been relegated to the garage or backyard or taken to the animal shelter. Shelters are full of dogs that were once welcomed into homes with excitement, but unfortunately, often without preparation or commitment.

Chapter Three

How to Choose a Dachshund

I t's easy to find a Dachshund—but it's not so easy to find the one that has all the characteristics you are looking for, that is, one with good health and temperament that not only looks like a Dachshund, but is the coat, size, and color you want. You want to find a Dachshund bred by somebody who is careful about the dogs they breed, the way they are raised, and the homes they go to.

Dachshund Coat Types

Variety is the spice of life, and Dachshunds, with their three official AKC varieties (and six in some other countries) are as spicy as they come. The varieties the AKC recognizes are based on the three different coat types, each of which was originally developed to hunt in slightly different conditions. Today the varieties still retain some differences in temperament because of crosses with other breeds.

The AKC recognizes the three coat types as separate varieties, which means they do not compete against each other as the same breed in shows, but can be bred together. However, in practice, most breeders do not inter-breed the coat varieties.

The Smooth Variety

Sassy and sleek, the Dachshund most of us grew up with is the familiar smooth variety. The AKC standard describes the coat as "short, smooth and shining." The hair should be neither long nor thick, but hug the body like a tight jacket, showing off the Dachshund's svelte physique.

Although early Dachshunds were a mixed bag when it came to coats, the smooth took the lead early on as the prototypical Dachshund. Its coat is simple to care for: an occasional bath when dirty, plus some brushing to remove dead hair, and she's good to go!

The Longhaired Variety

Glamorous and glistening, the longhaired Dachshund is the hot dog's answer to elegance. The luxurious long coat is longer under the neck, and on the forechest, the underside of the body, the ears, behind the legs, and beneath the tail. The hair is often slightly wavy, but should never be curly. It should not be so profuse that it obscures the body shape, nor should it be equally long all over, and especially not so long that it parts on the back.

Nobody knows how the longhaired Dachshund came about. It may have been selectively bred from the occasional longhairs produced from smooth Dachshunds. Because long hair is recessive to short, it's not uncommon for smooth-coated dogs to sometimes produce long-coated offspring. It's also possible that smooth Dachshunds, or even longhaired offspring of smooths, were purposefully bred with various spaniels. Longhaired Dachshunds are known as the lovers of the breed, more docile and spaniel-like in temperament than the other varieties.

Breed Truths

The MS, ML, and MW Designations

Many Dachshund names end with either the letter S, L, W, MS, ML, or MW. It's a code serious breeders use so that future generations will know the size and variety of a Dachshund in a pedigree. *S* stands for *smooth*, *L* for *long*, and *W* for *wire*. If these letters stand alone, the dog is a standard size Dachshund. *MS*, *ML*, and *MW* designate a miniature smooth, miniature longhaired, and miniature wirehaired, respectively.

Long coats were popular with hunters who wanted a dog with more protection from the cold. However, the coat tended to weigh the dog down in wet conditions, as it would get heavy with mud. It would also sometimes get stuck in brambles.

Because most people don't take their Dachshunds hunting in the mud, that shouldn't be a problem. The long coat needs to be bathed every month or so, and brushed once or twice a week. No trimming is required, but you may trim the paws to keep your dog from tracking in dirt.

The Wirehaired Variety

Dapper and dashing, the jaunty wirehaired Dachshund is the perfect blend of hound and terrier types. The body coat is uniformly tight, short, and thick. It's made up of a coarse, hard outer coat, with somewhat softer and shorter undercoat hairs beneath and between the outer coat's hairs. The ears are almost smooth, but the face is accented with a beard and eyebrows. The coat should be close-fitting enough that the dog retains the sleek body outline of the smooth. Hair should not be long, curly, wavy, or sticking up in all directions.

Early Dachshund descriptions occasionally included rough-coated dogs, but these were probably not the ancestors of present-day wires. These dogs were developed later, probably by purposefully crossing smooth Dachshunds with various hard-coated terriers and wirehaired pinschers. Wires are the mischief makers of the Dachshund breed, combining smooth Dachshund spunk with terrier attitude.

Wirehaireds are the most popular Dachshunds with people interested in hunting with them. The coat affords maximum protection against brambles and teeth, and because the wires have long been the hunting variety of choice in Germany, many top hunting wire Dachshunds around the world come directly from these German hunting wirehaireds.

The wire coat needs bathing every few months, and brushing or combing once a week. It also needs dead hairs to be pulled out of the coat every few months. Grooming the wire for show is the most difficult of the Dachshund varieties, but still not very hard.

Dachshund Sizes

Dachshunds originally came in different sizes not to satisfy different lap sizes, but to satisfy different hunting needs. Facing fierce badgers, confronting foxes, trailing deer, or hunting rabbits through thick underbrush all require Dachshunds of slightly different sizes.

Helpful Hints

Coat Genetics

Wire coat is dominant to smooth coat, which is in turn dominant to long coat. Other modifiers determine the exact length and texture.

In Germany, larger Dachshunds weighing about 15 to 20 pounds were better at jobs requiring them to face tough quarry, such as badgers and foxes. Slightly smaller Dachshunds, called Zwerg, or dwarf, Dachshunds,

FYI: Club Classifications

American Kennel Club	Standard: Usually 16–32 lb.	Miniature: 11 lb. and under	–
Kennel Club (England)	Standard: 20–26 lb.	Miniature: about 10 lb.	–
FCI (Germany, Northern Europe, South America)	Normalgrosse: (Up to about 20 lb.) Chest circumference: 35 cm	Dwarf (zwerg): – Chest circumference: 30–35 cm	Rabbit (Kaninichen): (<3.5 kg) Chest circumference: 30 cm

were preferred for trailing deer, where they needed to push through brush yet still cover long distances. These Dachshunds are the miniature Dachshunds we know today. Even smaller dogs, called Kaninchenteckels, were better for trailing rabbits through thickets. These smallest Dachshunds are still shown separately in Germany and most European countries, but not in America. At one time, the Kaninchenteckels were bred with various toy dogs to create lapdogs called Kaninchenhundes. Although they were popular around 1900, their popularity fell so much after a couple of decades that they ceased to exist.

In most of the world, Dachshund sizes are separated by weight at 12 months of age. However, in Germany and other countries regulated by the Federation Cynologique Internationale (FCI), they're separated by chest circumference at 18 months of age. The logic behind this is that it's the chest circumference that determines how large a hole or tightly-woven a thicket a dog can fit into.

In most countries, different sizes are shown as different varieties, just as the different coat types are shown as different varieties in AKC shows. However, the AKC does not separate the two sizes into varieties, despite requests from various Dachshund clubs and factions. With three coat types and two size types, that would create the problem of six varieties.

In recent years the popularity of miniatures has grown tremendously among pet owners, who value their more convenient size, especially for apartment living. Plus, they're cute!

Breed Truths

Tweenies

Serious breeders rarely interbreed the two sizes because of the high number of dogs produced that end up heavier than the miniature weight limit, yet lighter than the preferred weight for standards. Often referred to as "tweenies," they can't win in the show ring, but make wonderful companions.

Dachshund Coat Patterns and Colors

Patterns

Radiant red, brilliant black, or dazzling dapple—these are but a mere sample of the Dachshund palette of colors. Dachshunds have one of the greatest arrays of colors of any breed of dog. The color you see depends on the interplay of several genes for coat pattern and several genes for hair color, so it helps if you understand the basic choices before trying to understand all the combinations.

The two most common Dachshund patterns are self-colored and tan-pointed.

Self-colored A self-colored dog is basically one shade of red, from mahogany to cream, all over, like the familiar red Dachshund we all grew up with. In most breeds, this color is called *sable*, but in Dachshunds, the term sable is used to describe another pattern. Instead, self-colored Dachshunds are usually called red, black-fringed red, mahogany, or in some cases, cream. Black-fringed and mahogany dogs often have a darker stripe down the back, and are usually born very dark, gradually lightening with age.

Tan-pointed A tan-pointed dog has a dark body coat with tan on its legs, eyebrows, and muzzle, and under the tail (like the pattern seen in Doberman Pinschers). Whether a dog is self-colored or tan-pointed depends on genes at one gene location (the **a** locus), with the gene for self-coloration dominant to that for tan-pointed.

Clear Red Many self-colored dogs have black interspersed in their coats, including black fringes on their ear tips. They also have black whiskers. But some, called clear reds, have no black hairs at all, not even black whiskers. That's because of genes at an entirely different genetic location, the **e** locus. Two copies of the **e** gene prevent any black at all from forming in the coat or whiskers, whether the dog is otherwise self-colored or tan-pointed. No matter what the genes at the **a** location are telling the coat to do, a dog with two copies of **e** will be some shade of clear red to cream. It's this **e** gene that makes predicting coat patterns and colors hard to do!

Sable In most other breeds, the term *sable* is used for red dogs that have black hairs interspersed in their coat, such as many red Dachshunds do. But in Dachshunds, *sable* means a dog that has banded hairs, so that each hair is light near the body but dark at its tip. This banded effect usually occurs only on top of the dog's head, and the top and sides of its body. The dog's underside, face, and feet are entirely the lighter base color, and the face may have a widow's peak where the banded and non-banded hairs meet. The effect is that of a dog that is darker colored on the top of its body, gradually getting lighter toward the extremities. Sables are most often seen

Helpful Hints

Piebald or Double Dapple?

If a dapple dog is also piebald, it's extremely confusing to figure out if the dog is actually a piebald or a double dapple. You can look for a few hints, however. If both parents were dapples, or if piebalds are not on both the sire and dam's sides of the pedigree, the puppy has a strong possibility of being a double dapple. The best way to know for sure is through a DNA test that can detect the **M** gene. This test is available through GenMark (*www.genmarkag.com*).

in long coats. Because it's a dominant gene, only one parent need be a sable in order to produce a sable puppy.

Wild Boar It is likely that the pattern called wild boar, which is seen in wire coats (and occasionally smooth coats), is simply how the sable pattern looks on a wire coat. When the wild boar pattern is on a red background, the dog is said to be red boar.

Wheaten It is likely that the pattern called wheaten, which is seen only in wire coats, is simply how light reds and creams look on a wire coat.

Brindle Brindle-patterned Dachshunds, in which irregular dark vertical stripes overlie areas of tan or red, were rare several years ago, but have become more popular lately. A dominant gene can cause a dog to be brindle. If a dog is self-colored, the brindling will be over its entire body. If a dog has tan points, the brindling will be evident only on the tan.

Dapple Dapple Dachshunds are the pattern that is called merle in most other breeds. Dappling refers to irregular blotches of dark color overlaid on a lighter shade of that same color, with both dark and light areas often interspersed with white hairs. Dappling can be superimposed over other patterns, including tan points, in which case the points will usually be discernable and undappled. The extent varies so much that in some dogs, you have to really look before you find slight areas of dappling. Dapple dogs often have one or both eyes that are blue or blue flecked. The pattern is caused by one copy of the dominant gene, **M**. One parent must be a dapple to produce a dapple puppy.

Double Dapple Dogs with two copies of the **M** gene have the same type of merle patterning except that it usually has a lot more white. Although these dogs are stunning, they come with a higher risk of having visual

FYI: Colors and the Standard

The AKC Dachshund standard was rewritten regarding color in 2007 to clarify some points of contention. The following are now considered unacceptable according to the standard:
- piebald pattern
- double dapple pattern
- white anywhere on the dog other than a small area on the chest (a larger area is permissible on the chest of a dapple)
- total lack of tan or cream markings on black, blue, chocolate, or Isabella (mouse-gray) Dachshunds
- combination of dapple and brindle patterns on the same dog
- any blue in either eye of a brindle Dachshund (this indicates a combination of the dapple and brindle patterns)
- patterned or flesh-colored nose
- any nose color other than black on red, cream, black/tan, black/cream, wild boar, and red boar Dachshunds

and hearing problems. This is why it is not advisable to breed dapples to one another, or to buy a double dapple. If you are considering buying one, however, do so pending a hearing test and eye exam.

Piebald Piebald Dachshunds are white Dachshunds with colored spots. Some have large areas of white, whereas others have white only on their legs, tail tip, and collar. The piebald pattern is recessive to the nonpiebald pattern. When two piebalds are bred together, they can produce only piebalds.

The pattern can overlie any of the other colors and patterns. Think of a piebald as a dog that had a bucket of whitewash haphazardly thrown over him, so just parts of his original pattern and color show through. The Dachshund standards of European countries don't consider piebalds as acceptable for the show ring; however, it is an old pattern present in Dachshunds almost since the breed's inception.

Solid Black Some black and tan-pointed Dachshunds may appear to be black either because they have very tiny areas of tan, or because the tan is heavily brindled or very dark. But some may in fact be solid black. Solid black dogs are caused by a separate gene that is uncommon in Dachshunds. Solid black Dachshunds are not an acceptable pattern according to the AKC standard.

Coat Colors

Besides patterns, Dachshund coats come in different colors. All colors, however, are some variant of black or red. Black, gray or brown pigmentation is produced by the substance eumelanin in the hair shaft. Red or tan pigmentation is produced by the substance pheomelanin in the hair shaft. White coats are the result of a hair shaft with neither type of melanin in it.

Black and Its Variants

Black When eumelanin is not affected by other color genes that change or dilute it, the hair is black, such as the body coat in a black and tan Dachshund.

Brown The presence of two recessive genes at the **b** location will make any black on a dog turn out brown or liver instead. Even the nose and paw pads will be brown, and the eyes tend to be amber. The most common example is a chocolate and tan dog, which is a tan-pointed dog with brown, instead of black, hair. A brindle could also have brown stripes, though, and a dapple could be a chocolate dapple. Even a sable could be red with brown tips. Chocolate does not significantly affect the saturation of any red hair on the dog. Occasionally a clear red or cream dog that has two **e** genes (thus preventing the expression of eumelanin) will

DNA Tests for Pattern and Color

A DNA test exists that can tell you whether your Dachshund carries the genes for
- self-color versus tan-pointed at the **a** locus
- mahogany versus clear red at the **e** locus
- black versus brown at the **b** locus
- the merle gene, whether one or two copies

More tests are being developed for other patterns and colors. The widest selection can be found at *www.vetgen.com*.

have two brown genes, but the only way you can tell is that the nose is brown and the eyes may be light.

Blue The presence of two recessive genes at the **d** location will make any black on a dog turn out gray, or "blue," instead. Even the nose and paw pads will be slate colored, and the eyes somewhat lighter. The most common example is a blue and tan dog, but it can also turn the stripes of a brindle gray, and can affect any hair that would otherwise be black. Blue dilution does not affect the saturation of any red hair on the dog. In some breeds, the blue coat coloration is associated with thin, fragile hair and skin problems, but this does not seem to be the case with Dachshunds.

Isabella The presence of two recessive genes at both the **b** and **d** locations will make any black turn out grayish tan or fawn. This color is most noticeable on a tan-pointed dog; however, Isabellas are uncommon and generally not sought after. In many breeds, they have coat and skin problems, but again, this does not seem to be the case with Dachshunds.

Red and Its Variants

Red Red coats are produced by the substance pheomelanin in the hair shaft. When this pheomelanin is not affected by other color genes that dilute it, the hair is red. Red is most noticeable in self-colored Dachshunds, but it's also apparent in the points of tan-pointed dogs.

Gold The depth of red is affected by various other genes, which determine whether the hair will be deep red, medium red, or gold. In general, more saturated colors are dominant. In self-colored dogs, the saturation is obvious, but it can also be seen in the tan areas of tan-pointed dogs.

Cream Creams can be produced in two different ways. One is caused by the effects of diluting genes that dilute the color even past gold. In such cases, the dilution can sometimes also affect the nose, and the nose tends to be light. These dogs will often darken as they age. They may or may not have black whiskers. In tan-pointed dogs, the points will appear very light.

FYI: Breeders Compared

Source	Definition	Price
Hobby breeder	Produces for competition	$$$
Companion breeder	Produces for pets	$$
Backyard breeder	Produces for fun or profit	$
Backyard mill	Produces for profit	$$$

The Sources Compared

Why do you want a good breeder? Besides being your best source of a puppy with good health, good temperament, and good looks, a good breeder will be a mentor and friend. You can get a wonderful Dachshund companion from any source, but you have a better chance of getting a healthy one from a reputable source.

No matter what source you are considering, ask them the 10 questions on page 46. A good source will have appropriate answers to all 10 questions. An acceptable source will have appropriate answers to at least seven questions. A poor source will have acceptable answers to five or fewer questions, or will say they don't apply.

Newspaper Ads

The classifieds section was once the major source for puppy buyers. Most people who place such ads are backyard breeders, typically families with one or two Dachshunds they in turn bought from a newspaper ad. Be warned that there is a risk that these people may not know everything about breeding heathy, well-socialized puppies. It is important to investigate the sources and ask to see the puppy's medical and immunization records. The puppies may not be great quality, but they are generally good companions.

Internet Ads

The Internet has sprung up as a huge selling ground for puppies. Backyard breeders who used to sell a litter or two a year have discovered they can sell lots of litters through the Internet. Web sites claim they are Dachshund experts and sell as many puppies as they can. Be wary of breeders who do not advertise titled parents or health testing, but instead have lots of "cute" puppy pictures. Again, investigate the source, and make sure you are purchasing from a reputable breeder.

Pros	Quality
High quality, health tested, better follow-up	high
May be health tested	medium
Often home raised, short wait	low
Short wait	very low

Hobby Breeders

Many hobby breeders also have web sites. The difference is that they seldom advertise on the all-breed "puppies for sale" sites. Their web sites emphasize the achievements of their adults, not the cuteness of their puppies. They often include extensive information on Dachshund care, health, and temperament. Such hobby breeders produce only a few litters a year, with the goal being to improve their line. Not every puppy will be a great show dog; however, these puppies are sold as pets. These pets receive the same care as their next-champion prospects, and are usually sold for affordable prices if your home is deemed appropriate. You can find hobby breeders through Dachshund clubs and shows (see "Looking for Love").

Companion Breeders

A difficult type of breeder to classify is the companion breeder. Done well, this breeder fills the gap between hobby breeders and backyard breeders, producing health-tested and well-socialized puppies as companions, rather than as show dogs.

Helpful Hints

Colors and Registration Papers

The AKC allows you to register only one color and one pattern for your Dachshund, even though your dog may be a combination of patterns. For example, a dog could be a chocolate and tan-pointed brindle. That's why you can't always rely on pedigree information to trace colors and patterns.

Looking for Love

The Dachshund Club of America (DCA) breeder list, available online at *www. dachshund-dca.org/kennelads.html*, is a good place to find hobby breeders. These breeders are all members of the DCA and have agreed to abide by the club code of ethics. Although the items of this code are not enforceable, they do at least speak to a minimal standard to which all breeders should comply.

BE PREPARED! 10 Questions to Ask Your Breeder

Ask these questions of any prospective breeder:

1. Do you specialize in Dachshunds? Good breeders work with only one or two breeds of dogs, so they can concentrate on just those breeds.

2. Do you have litters available all the time? Good breeders seldom breed more than three or four litters per year, so they can concentrate on those litters.

3. Can I visit in person? Good breeders are proud of their dogs and facilities. If you can't visit, it could be because they don't want you to see either.

4. Can I meet the dam? Good breeders have the dam available. The sire, however, may live elsewhere.

5. How did you choose these parents? Good breeders should be able to discuss the merits and possible shortcomings of both parents, and why they chose to breed them.

6. Can I see the pedigree? Good breeders have the pedigree on hand, without searching or sending for it. In fact, good breeders will also have pictures and knowledge of many of the dogs in the pedigree for several generations back.

7. Are the puppies registered? Good breeders will have AKC-registered dogs (or their dogs will be registered with the national kennel club in whatever country they're in). The United Kennel Club is the only other acceptable registry in the United States.

8. Is there a written sales agreement? Good breeders will supply a written agreement that includes the registration information, price, and any warranty or conditions.

9. Is there a health warranty? Good breeders will guarantee the puppy's health, barring accident, for about a week after you've taken possession and under certain conditions. They will not, however, guarantee it for years, because nobody can make such a promise. As with all living beings, dogs can become prematurely ill, and can suffer from unforeseen hereditary problems. A good breeder does her best to avoid them, but cannot guarantee they won't happen.

10. What do you need from me? Good breeders ask for more than money. In fact, that's the last thing they mention. They want evidence that you're going to provide a good home for their puppy for life.

Among the items mentioned in the DCA Code of Ethics are that each breeder should devote herself to the betterment of the breed; that accurate records be kept of all breedings and registrations; to accept full responsibility for every dog bred; to sell with a contract that ensures the breeder is contacted should the owner not be able to keep the dog and to assist in the placement of that dog; and to sell dogs with written bills of sale detailing registration information, pedigree, medical history, terms of sale, and instructions for feeding and care.

Local Dachshund clubs (*www.dachshund-dca.org/clubs.html*) can also be a valuable source of information about upcoming litters and events. Having a local breeder is a great advantage, because you can get to know the breeders and their dogs first-hand, and they also can get to know you. Having your breeder close by is especially helpful for advice and just for having an extended Dachshund family.

If no local Dachshund clubs are nearby, you may be able to find an all-breed club (you can locate one near you by going to *www.akc.org*, then clicking on Clubs, then Club Search). You can join a local club or simply attend a local dog show (find these by going to *www.akc.org*, then clicking on Events, then Event and Awards Search). The premier Dachshund show is the national specialty show, held in a different state each year. It's almost a week's worth of hundreds of Dachshunds doing almost everything Dachshunds do. To find the date and location, go to *www.dachshund-dca.org*. By attending a show you can meet Dachshund exhibitors and make arrangements to talk later, after they've shown their dogs. You'll also get to meet lots of Dachs!

You can also find good breeders in Dachshund and all-breed dog magazines such as *Dog World*. You can join one of the many Internet Dachshund discussion lists and get to know breeders there.

Choose a Choosy Breeder

One way to evaluate breeders is to compare how they evaluate you. Good breeders are choosy about where their puppies go. They make sure their puppies will go to homes where they will be loved for a lifetime. They know that Dachshunds require special people, and that any dog requires a lot of commitment and work. They are too familiar with people who make big promises but are not really prepared for Dachshund ownership. Good breeders will ask about your experience with dogs and with Dachshunds in particular. They will ask about your facilities and family. They will discuss expenses, exercise, training, grooming, health care, and safety issues with you. They usually require that you neuter or spay your dog. They may ask you to wait for several months for a litter; during this "cooling off" period they can make sure you are not just buying on impulse. If a breeder doesn't care where their puppies are going, they probably don't care where they came from either, and there's a good chance very little thought went into breeding and raising the litter.

Breed Needs

What Age?

The best time to bring a new puppy home is between eight and twelve weeks of age. Before seven weeks, removing a puppy from its dam and littermates deprives it of learning essential canine social skills. After twelve weeks, puppies naturally become more fearful of new situations. However, if the breeder has taken measures to expose the puppy to new experiences and people, an older puppy can make the transition just fine. Don't hesitate to welcome a well-adjusted Dachshund of any age into your home. In fact, an adult Dachshund is a great choice if you value your furniture, rugs, and sanity.

Puppy Checklist

Dachshunds are among dogdom's most heart-stealing puppies. That's a problem if you're trying to remain objective, because once you hold one, you'll have a hard time putting him down. That's why you really should visit the breeder with the idea of leaving puppyless and making your final decision without those soulful eyes pleading to go home with you. Good luck with that!

While you are with the pups, steel yourself to make an honest evaluation of them. Dachshund puppies sleep hard and play hard, so if they are sleeping, you may have to wait to see them at their best. They should be friendly toward you; avoid any that are shy or overly independent. Their eyes, ears, and nose should be free of discharge, and they should show no signs of diarrhea.

Make any sale contingent upon a veterinary examination within two to three days. Your veterinarian is in the best position to evaluate the puppy's health. The breeder should have supplied the puppy's vaccinations and worming records.

CHECKLIST

Puppy Health Check

✔ Before getting attached to any puppy, give him a quick health check.

✔ The skin should not have parasites, hair loss, crusts, or reddened areas.

✔ The eyes, ears, and nose should be free of discharge.

✔ Puppies should not be coughing, sneezing, or vomiting.

✔ The area around the anus should have no hint of irritation or recent diarrhea.

✔ Puppies should be neither thin nor potbellied.

✔ The gums should be pink, not pale.

✔ The eyelids and lashes should not fold in on the eyes.

✔ By the age of 10 weeks, males should have both testicles descended into the scrotum.

✔ Avoid any puppy that is making significant breathing sounds, including excessive wheezing or snorting.

✔ You should make any sale contingent on a veterinary exam performed within two to three days.

Puppy Personality Testing

Dachshund puppies should have many of the same personality traits that adults have. They should be playful, alert, curious, and self-confident. They may not be the most obedient puppies you've ever seen—remember, they are Dachshunds—but they should be at least somewhat responsive to you.

Traditional hunting Dachshunds need that spark of independence to follow their noses, but chances are, you want your dog mostly as a companion, so you may opt for a little less independence than is traditional.

No matter what, avoid puppies that growl or snap at you, or ones that freeze, cringe, or urinate when you pick them up. You want a puppy that enjoys being with her littermates, but enjoys being with you even more. But remember, puppies don't stay awake for long periods at a time, so don't expect them to keep on playing while you make up your mind. In fact, if only one is left standing, that might be one to avoid—unless you want an exceptionally energetic dog!

PERSONALITY POINTERS
Puppy Aptitude Test

Test/Purpose	How to Test
Social Attraction Measures sociability and dependence	The tester coaxes the puppy toward her.
Following Measures dependence versus independence	The tester walks away.
Restraint Measures dominance versus submissiveness	The tester gently rolls the puppy on its back and holds it there.
Social Dominance Measures dominance versus submissiveness	The tester strokes the standing puppy on the back.
Elevation Dominance Measures acceptance of dominance when the puppy has no control	The tester lifts the pup slightly off the ground and holds it there.
Retrieving	The tester tosses a crumpled-up piece of paper.
Sound Sensitivity	The tester makes a sharp noise a few feet from the puppy.
Touch Sensitivity	The tester presses the webbing between the toes.
Sight Sensitivity	The tester jerks a towel on a string near the puppy.

There's nothing wrong with choosing the puppy that seems to choose you, or with letting the breeder choose the puppy. After all, there's no way you can get to know them as well as the breeder knows them in the short time you'll be there.

Puppy Aptitude Tests

Many breeders and puppy buyers place great confidence in aptitude testing when it comes to choosing puppies. Puppy aptitude tests were developed for choosing the best candidates for guide dogs, and since that time have been modified for companion dogs.

Puppy aptitude tests can give you a hint of how the puppies in a litter measure up against each other and puppies from other litters. Optimally, they are given as close to when the puppy is 49 days old as possible, and

What to Look For	Results
Does the puppy come eagerly, eventually, or not at all?	The faster the puppy comes, the better.
Does the puppy follow eagerly, hesitantly, or not at all?	The more eagerly the puppy follows, the better.
Does the puppy fight it, eventually relax, or give up immediately?	The more a puppy fights, the greater its tendency to be dominant.
Does the puppy protest, lick the tester, try to escape, or roll over?	An intermediate response is usually best.
Does the puppy struggle fiercely, accept it, try to lick, or freeze?	An intermediate response is usually best.
Does the pup fetch it, grab it and run away, or just look?	A pup that runs after it and brings it back is a better dog for retrieving.
Does the puppy bark at it, look at it, or cringe?	Barking or looking are good responses.
How long does it take the puppy to protest?	A medium sensitivity is probably best.
Does the puppy give chase, just look, or run away?	A puppy that looks is probably best for most pets.

the tester should be a stranger to the puppy. If your heart is set on a puppy but the test says otherwise, come back and try him again. The tests are far from infallible, and in fact, probably don't have that much predictive value for adult behavior. But they can evaluate the puppy at the time in his life you take him home. And they're fun! The test consists of nine parts.

Rescue

Dachshunds find themselves homeless for many reasons. Most often it's just a case of the wrong home for the right dog, or the wrong circumstances even for the right home. Rescue Dachshunds come in all ages, from all circumstances, and in all conditions. Occasionally entire litters come to rescue,

FYI: Rescue Resources

Almost Home Dachshund Rescue Society: www.almosthomerescue.org

Dachshund Adoption and Rescue: www.daretorescue.com

Dachshund Rescue of North America: www.drna.org

Dachshund Rescue Web Page: http://dachshund-rescue.org

Coast to Coast Dachshund Rescue: www.c2cdr.org

List of local Dachshund rescue groups: www.dachshund-dca.org/rescue.html

National database of dogs in shelters: www.petfinder.com

sometimes ancient dogs who seek only a secure home in which to spend their last days. Many rescues have been cherished companions and are suddenly alone in the world. Other rescues may have been discarded puppy-mill breeding stock who have lived out their reproductive usefulness. Some rescues have never lived in a house before, or known a gentle touch or kind word. Regardless, rescues are often apprehensive, confused, and even frightened. They may cling to their foster owners or new families, as though afraid they will lose their beacon of hope. With time, training, and security they gradually adapt to their new circumstances and become exceptional family companions.

Rescue dogs need secure, permanent homes where they won't be given up again. That's one reason rescue groups are picky about where these dogs go. You may be asked to provide veterinary references, and the rescue group may schedule a phone interview or home visit. Many rescue groups provide temperament testing, basic training, and behavior consultation. Adopting from a rescue group provides new owners with a safety net should problems arise. They also often provide opportunities to become club members, participate in Dachshund activities and rescue reunions, and even become part of the rescue team.

Rescue dogs are not free. Not only do people tend to value objects or pets they have an investment in more than those they don't, but rescue groups need to charge a reasonable fee to recoup their expenses and continue to provide services. Some rescues are less expensive than others, however. Generally, Dachshunds from county shelters are the least expensive, whereas those from Dachshund rescue groups cost more. Dogs from the latter, however, are usually examined for health and temperament problems, and treated as needed, so that the costs even out. Regardless, a rescue Dachshund is the deal of a lifetime.

Dachshund Breeding

As you're visiting breeders, you may start wondering whether this is something you'd like to do yourself. Breeding a litter is a big commitment and a big decision. Breeding your female entails some health risk to her. Although most birthings go just fine, some dams require a Caesarean section to deliver the puppies and could in fact die without one. After whelping, complications such as mastitis and eclampsia can be painful or fatal. This is not the way to introduce the kids to the miracle of life.

Breed Truths

Which Sex?

Have you considered males versus females? In Dachshunds, the difference isn't great. The males are a bit larger, and some consider them a bit more loving. Unless you have her spayed, a female will come in estrus twice a year, which can be messy and troublesome. Unless castrated, a male is more likely to lift his leg on furniture to mark with urine. If you already have a dog, often the best choice is a dog of the opposite sex—as long as you plan to neuter or spay it.

Before you decide to breed, ask yourself these questions:

1. Do I meet the same requirements for a good breeder? (See page 46.)
2. Can I find good homes for these puppies whose lives will depend on the choices I make?
3. If new owners can no longer keep the puppy, can I commit to taking him back?
4. Do I have the facilities to raise a litter where they can be safe and happy?
5. Do I have the time to clean up after and socialize a litter? What if the puppies are orphaned or need to be hand-raised?
6. Do I have the money to pay for health clearances, stud service, pre-breeding exams, any whelping emergencies, food, vaccinations, and worming?
7. Is my female sound in mind and body? Is she free of back problems? In good weight?
8. Is she a better-than-average representative of the breed?

In 2007, more than 36,000 Dachshunds were registered with the AKC. That doesn't count the probably equal number that were bred but not registered. There is no Dachshund shortage in the world, so don't think you need to do your part by breeding a litter. In fact, so many Dachshunds end up in rescue every year that you're really doing your part for the breed by not breeding a litter.

Chapter Four

Caring for a Puppy

Getting a new puppy is exciting. Fortunately, there's plenty to do while you await the big day. There are rooms to puppy-proof, things to buy, and adventures to anticipate!

Crate Training

Every dog should be crate trained. A crate gives your dog a secure bed of his own and gives you a place to put him where you won't worry about him. Crates help inhouse training, provide a safe means of car travel, and provide a safe haven when staying with friends or at hotels. A crate-trained dog will fare better if he has to be crated at the veterinary hospital or if he must have bed rest at home—especially important for Dachshunds with bad backs.

But crates can be overused. They are not a place for your dog to languish while you entertain yourself with other things. Overuse of crates can create serious behavioral problems. Think of a crate as your child's crib. It's a safe place to sleep, but not a place to grow up. And it's certainly not a place for punishment.

Establish a good association with the crate by feeding your dog in it. At first just place the food slightly inside the crate so he doesn't even have to go inside to eat. Then move it farther inside. Finally, close the door while he eats, opening it as soon as he finishes. You can probably do this within the period of a day. Soon he will be running to the crate as soon as he sees you with food. If you want, you can now introduce a cue, such as "Bedtime!" for him to go in the crate.

You can extend his time in the crate by giving him chew toys or interactive toys to occupy him while inside. Extend his time gradually, always trying to let him out before he has a chance to get bored or vocal. If he does begin to protest, wait until he is momentarily quiet before letting him out. Continue to extend the time he must be quiet before he gets released.

The crate is one of the safest spots your Dachshund puppy can be, but you must do your part. Do not leave collars on puppies while they are in their crates. Collars, especially choke collars or collars with tags, can get caught in crate wires, and puppies have a bad habit of getting their lower jaws somehow stuck in loose collars. Soft bedding is wonderful for most puppies,

CHECKLIST

Puppy-Proofing

Check all over your house for

- ✔ uncovered electrical outlets—can cause shocks
- ✔ open stairways, decks, or balconies—can cause falls
- ✔ unsecured doors—can allow escapes or slam shut on puppy
- ✔ open cabinets holding cleaners and degreasers—can invite poisoning
- ✔ accessible garbage pails holding enticing rancid food and splintering bones—can invite poisoning, sickness, or injury to gut
- ✔ plastic wraps that can be swallowed—can lodge in intestines
- ✔ hanging table cloths that if pulled, can bring dishes crashing down—can injure puppy by hitting him on the head or back
- ✔ swinging doors—can trap a puppy's head and neck
- ✔ fireplace without a secure fire screen—can burn puppy
- ✔ unsteady bookcases—can fall on and crush puppy
- ✔ craft or sewing kits—needles and threads can be swallowed, causing severe injury and illness
- ✔ heavy statues or vases—can fall on puppy
- ✔ children's toys—can chew off and swallow pieces
- ✔ open closets, especially shoe closets—can chew up your shoes and make you mad
- ✔ pills and medicines—takes only a small amount to poison a puppy
- ✔ hair treatments—can poison or cause eye injuries

- ✔ drain cleaners—can poison or cause eye injuries
- ✔ razors—can be swallowed, cutting up mouth and gut
- ✔ diaper pails—disposable diapers can be eaten and can swell in stomach
- ✔ antifreeze—tastes sweet, but even one swallow can cause fatal kidney failure
- ✔ fuels, cleaners, paints—can be toxic
- ✔ batteries—battery acid can be toxic
- ✔ nails and screws—can be swallowed and become lodged in intestines
- ✔ herbicides, insecticides, and fertilizers—can be toxic
- ✔ rodent bait—can be enticing to eat, but fatal

Check all over your yard for

- ✔ weak fence—can allow your puppy to escape and be harmed
- ✔ rotted limbs—can fall on puppy
- ✔ unfenced pool—can drown puppy; always have a way for a dog to climb out, and teach him to find and use it
- ✔ cocoa mulch—contains theobromine, which is poisonous to dogs
- ✔ fruit and nut trees—some nuts and fruit parts are poisonous; they can also fall on a puppy's head
- ✔ pointed sticks at eye level—can poke into a running puppy's eye
- ✔ predators—can go off with a small dog
- ✔ treated lawns—can be treated with toxic chemicals that the puppy may lick off his paws
- ✔ poisonous plants—can be eaten
- ✔ insect hives—digging or playing puppy can cause them to attack

but those that chew and swallow it may have to be relegated to surfaces less likely to cause intestinal blockages. If your puppy tends to chew on the wire, he could get his jaw or tooth caught. Discourage such behavior by spraying the wire with anti-chew preparations and by making sure your pup has no issues with being crated.

House Training

The best time to start teaching your Dachshund where to potty is between seven and nine weeks of age. Before that time, pups don't appear to be able to either grasp the idea or control themselves sufficiently. After nine weeks of age, puppies seem to prefer using whatever surface or place they were using between seven and nine weeks of age. So it is very important that you make sure your pup has as few chances to go in the wrong places, and as many chances to go in the right places, as possible during this crucial time.

The typical dog owner pushes the pup out the door and shoves it closed behind him, leaving him all alone. The puppy protests, cries, and does just about everything but potty. Once let back inside, though, he relaxes enough to wet all over the floor. No matter how busy you are, early potty training must be a team sport. It must not, however, be playtime. Ignore the pup's attempts to play until he does his duty. Otherwise he will learn that potty time is playtime, and going outside with him will be counterproductive.

Breed Needs

Home Alone

It's natural for a young pup to seek parental security. Your pup is hard-wired to become anxious if he finds himself separated from his care-giver. A puppy that finds himself all alone will give out a distress vocal-ization, which brings his mother on the run. If nobody shows up, he will keep crying until he is too exhausted to continue. Naïve own-ers may think he has gotten over his angst, but exhaustion is not the same as being OK.

Giving your pup something to occupy him and comfort him while you are gone is useful, but it depends on what you give. Studies have shown that mirrors and soft, cuddly toys are most effective at calming separated puppies, but food has little value—probably because distressed puppies are not hungry puppies. Puppies are comforted by soft, warm, dog-shaped toys that even have a heartbeat, simulating the pup's littermates or dam.

Outdoor Rewards

There's another reason you need to be outside. Puppies are more likely to use the potty when they get praise and sometimes, treats, for doing it in the right place. Keep a jar of treats by the door and grab a handful when you go outside with him. Wait until he's just finishing, then heap on the praise and give him a treat. Don't wait until you're back inside; that's too late. Remember, it's inconvenient to the puppy to go outside; you have to make the reward worth that effort.

HOME BASICS
Gotta go!

Be responsive to your dog's cues and schedules.

- Immediately after a puppy awakens, he must potty.
- Within 15 minutes after eating, he must potty (the act of eating puts into motion all sorts of peristaltic gut motility).
- In the middle of playing, he must potty—a lot.
- If he exercises a lot, he'll drink a lot more water, and a while later he'll also have to urinate.
- If he starts whining for no reason, he has a reason, and it's going to smell bad unless you get him outside.
- When you see him sniffing and circling, he's going to go. Get him outside as fast as possible, even if you must carry him there.
- When in doubt, take him out!

Keep on Schedule

A regular schedule is important for training puppies. Besides going when he awakens, after he eats, and before he goes to bed, your pup will profit from being taken out at regular intervals. A standard rule of thumb is that a puppy can hold himself for as many hours as he is months old, within reason. Once he reaches five months of age, he's at his limit until adulthood, when he can last six to eight hours. Even when younger he can occasionally go longer, for instance, overnight, if you don't let him eat or guzzle down water before bed. That in turn means not encouraging vigorous play, which will make him thirsty, before bedtime. You don't wish to withhold water; just make sure he has no reason to drink a lot of it before bed.

You can help your puppy to have a regular bowel movement by feeding him on schedule and making sure you don't give him novel foods that may cause diarrhea.

Oops

Accidents will happen. Your reaction will determine if they happen more or less. Rubbing your dog's nose in a mess, no matter how recently it was deposited, doesn't do anything but make him less kissable and convince him you're strange. Such overzealous corrections, including yelling and spanking, when a puppy goes in the wrong place can work against your housetraining efforts in several ways. First, your dog seldom knows why you're on a rant and it causes him to distrust you. Second, your unpredictable nature causes him to be nervous, which in turn increases the likelihood he

will have to urinate or defecate. Third, if he figures out that it's his pottying that gets you upset, he will avoid doing it anywhere you can see him, including outdoors. Instead, he'll wait until he can sneak into another room where he can do it safely.

That doesn't mean you just ignore your dog if you catch him in the act. Give a startling "No!" or "Aght!" and scoop him up to scuttle him outside as quickly as possible. Once outside, be sure to reward him when he goes in the right place.

If you can't be home to take him out as often as he needs to go, use puppy urine pads (ask for puppy pee pads in the pet store) or sod sections as an indoor potty area. These can be moved outdoors once soiled to teach your puppy to go there. Newspapers are all right in a pinch, but they aren't absorbent.

House Training and Confinement

Young puppies avoid eliminating in their sleeping and eating area, so if you restrict your puppy to a small area, he's less likely to potty there. That way he'll actually make an effort to hold himself until you let him out. You can use the crate as his small area, making sure it's not so large that he can simply use one half of it for his bathroom. You can block off an overly large crate with a box or divider. You must let the puppy out of the crate regularly,

because if you force him to have accidents in it, he'll give up trying to hold it at all. Besides, it's inhumane to keep him crated for overly long periods.

Confine your pup when you can't supervise him. Let him out often, immediately taking him to his potty area. Once he's pottied, don't put him back in the crate. Use the time to socialize, play, snuggle, and do all the fun things that make having a puppy worth all the work.

Once he's house trained using the crate, expand his den area by placing his bed or crate in a tiny enclosed area—an area only a couple of feet beyond the boundary of his bed. Do everything you can to prevent him from soiling this area; that is, keep him on a frequent outdoor potty-break schedule. Gradually expand his area as he goes without soiling it, until eventually he has access to an entire room, or more.

Dachshund Development

This next year will bring incredible changes to your puppy, physically, behaviorally, and socially. Your role changes as he develops, and you need to know when he's old enough to train, or what kind of play is best for his age.

The following is what to expect from your puppy at different stages of development.

Newborn: Birth–Seven Weeks

Physical Development
- His smell and taste are developed, but his eyes and ears are closed until almost two weeks of age.
- Teeth begin to emerge at three weeks of age, starting with canines. By eight weeks, all 28 baby teeth are in.

Socialization
- For the first three weeks he prefers his dam to anyone.
- By four weeks he prefers his littermates. Playing with them teaches him to relate to other dogs, and may be important for learning to inhibit his bites.
- Once people begin to feed him, he begins to attend more to them.
- By seven weeks, he actively prefers people to his dam.

Behaviors
- He starts to eat semi-solid food by three weeks, and by five weeks is eating mostly solid food. The food he eats now will have a long-lasting influence on his adult preferences. If he eats only one food, he'll be cautious of novel foods. If he eats a variety, he'll prefer a variety.
- His dam no longer cleans up his wastes after he starts eating solid food. If he can, he'll totter away from his sleeping spot to do his duty. He's too young to learn house-training concepts.
- By seven weeks of age he's starting to be a little more cautious about new places and new things. He knows one person from another, and prefers those he knows. He can learn simple commands.

Care and Experiences
- He needs to explore while he's still fearless. Good experiences at this age will stay with him throughout life, helping him take new situations in stride later on.
- It's a good idea if he has practice sleeping by himself for short stretches. A little crate or bed is perfect for learning to sleep alone, or with a cuddly, warm toy.

Training
- As with human babies, early stimulation is vital for development.
- He can learn some simple commands. The first commands he learns will tend to be his "go-to" commands for the rest of his life; when he wants something, or is confused about what you want, he'll tend to "go to" that behavior. Stick with the standards, like sitting.
- Try some simple leash training. Use a lightweight cat leash. Just put on the leash and let him lead you around. Then entice him a few feet in the direction you want to go by dangling a treat just in front of him. Give it to him when he walks there.

Play
- Be sure to introduce balls and other toys to him, since puppies also learn specific play habits at an early age.

Infancy: Eight–Twelve Weeks

Physical Development
- All 28 of his baby teeth are in.
- His vision and hearing are almost adult-like, but not quite. They won't be fully mature until he's 10 weeks old.
- If he's a boy, both his testicles should be in his scrotum by now. If they're not, and he's destined for the show ring, it's time to consult with your veterinarian, because two normally descended testicles are required.

Socialization
- Starting at around seven or eight weeks, puppies begin to gradually become more fearful of novel situations, until by 12 weeks, they are more distrustful than trustful. That means you need to expose your puppy to as many situations as he'll encounter later in life as you can before this deadline.

Behaviors
- Bonding with his canine family has reached its highest point at seven weeks of age. It will gradually decline until he's 10 weeks old, after which he will prefer you.

Care and Experiences
- After nine weeks of age, puppies seem to cling to whatever substrate they learned to use for pottying between seven and nine weeks of age. Make sure that during this crucial time he's using whatever you want him to use for the rest of his life.
- Expose him to being alone for short periods. If you wait until he's 12 weeks, studies have shown he will have a much more difficult time adjusting. Exposure should be for very short time periods, before he has a chance to become stressed.
- He should get his first puppy vaccinations at around eight weeks.

Training
- He is eager to learn, and works well for either food or play.
- Now is the time to enroll him in puppy kindergarten class.

Play
- Now is the time to introduce him to the concept of fetch. Puppies not exposed to the idea of fetch at that early age have difficulty understanding it later.

Juvenile: Three–Six Months

Physical Development

- Around four to five months his baby teeth start to be replaced by adult teeth. His small front teeth will fall out and be replaced by permanent teeth first, followed by his canine teeth and finally his rear teeth. Sometimes the baby canine teeth don't fall out and the new ones come in beside them. If they stay there for more than a few days or a week, it could cause the new teeth to come in crooked and even adversely affect his occlusion, so you should consult your veterinarian.
- If you plan to neuter or spay your dog, the best time is at about five months of age, giving the dog time to mature but avoiding the chance of doing it after sexual maturity. Spaying before the first estrus greatly reduces the chance of breast cancer in later life.
- He's getting more coordinated, and much faster. He's making one of the grandest discoveries of his short life: You can't catch him!

Socialization

- By 12 weeks of age his tendency to be cautious of new things has overwhelmed his tendency to be curious about them, and that tendency will increase for the next few months. That doesn't mean he should be sheltered. He needs to continue being exposed to new people, places, and things, taking extra care to make sure he has good experiences. You may have to take things more slowly than you could have at a younger age.
- Social positions with any littermates gradually become more stable until the ranking order is fairly constant by week 16.

Behaviors

- His play is getting rougher and he's using his mouth on everything. Handing him a toy often distracts him from chewing on you, but if not, do what his littermate would do when he plays too rough: Say "ouch," and refuse to play until he calms down.
- He still objects to being separated from his family, whether canine or human. Keep giving him short periods alone. Studies have shown that soft stuffed toys, warm toys with a heartbeat, or a safe mirror can help alleviate his distress somewhat.

Care and Experiences

- Time to do another home check to make sure your place is still puppy-proofed for this dog that is bigger and more adventurous than the one you brought home.
- He's only now entering his heavy chewing stage. His baby teeth were capable of decorating everything with tiny pinprick holes, but his adult teeth can do a lot more damage.
- It's not unusual for him to regress when it comes to potty habits. Don't ask your three-month-old to hold himself for more than three hours. Less, if he's been playing or drinking a lot.

HOME BASICS
Chewing

Puppies chew, not only when they are teething, but at least until they're a year old. When you find your pup chewing on your belongings, take the object from him and replace it with a more acceptable object. Make sure the object you give him in exchange does not resemble anything of yours you don't want him to chew. That means no old shoes! No socks, no stuffed animals (if you have children who collect them), no carpet remnants, nothing that resembles anything he can find around the house. What your puppy learns to chew on at an early age will tend to be what he looks for to chew on for the rest of his life.

Assemble a group of dog toys and let your pup have only a few at a time, rotating them every few days so he has the excitement of new toys. Be sure to include some interactive toys, such as those he must work at to extract food. You can fill these with bones, soft cheese, canned dog food, or peanut butter, and then freeze them to make them last even longer. Some toys dispense kibble a piece at a time as the toy is rolled. Some toys are meant to be soaked in water and frozen, providing your pup a cold teething toy. With luck, your pup will prefer these fancy toys to your fancy belongings.

- He will need additional puppy vaccinations, and he should get his rabies vaccination at about 16 weeks (or younger, depending on state law).

Training
- At no other time in your puppy's life is he more amenable to training, but by about four months of age the ease with which puppies learn starts to decline. Be sure you've introduced him to the concept of learning before then.
- He can easily learn how to sit, lie down, stay, come, and heel by four months of age. If you have aspirations to compete in advanced obedience, or in agility, hunting, or trailing, now's the time to introduce him to the concepts of climbing over and under objects, and of using his nose to seek out hidden objects.
- Now is the time to enroll in an elementary puppy-training class.

Play
- His games still center around play fighting, but you need to redirect his games to something more cooperative. Try some fetch; if he won't bring the ball back, practice in a hallway. Use two balls, stand midway down the hall, and throw one ball to one end. Once he gets it, encourage him to come back—use a treat if you have to—and when he gets to you, throw the other ball in the other direction. Keep it up until he knows his reward for bringing you one ball is the chance to chase another.

- He's ready for some more sophisticated toys. Various puzzle and interactive toys require him to work to get treats or toys out of them. Such toys are great for occupying his mind when you can't be with him.

Adolescent: Seven–Twelve Months

Physical Development

- He's reached his adult size by now, although he still has some filling out to do.
- All 42 adult teeth should be in by seven months. Any baby teeth remaining should have been examined by a veterinarian long ago. Always X-ray before pulling baby teeth, because not all dogs have permanent ones waiting to erupt in their place.
- Testicles should be permanently in place. If one or both testicles still haven't descended, it's time to talk to your vet about what to do. At this age, the chance of them coming down is remote. It's not that they're not there; they're retained within his body, where the higher temperature renders them both incapable of creating viable sperm and more likely to become cancerous later in life. For this reason he'll probably need surgery to remove them.
- If not neutered or spayed, your Dachshund is becoming sexually mature. If male, his testicles are growing in size, and his penis, too, and he's showing interest in females in heat. He can probably sire puppies by nine months of age. Females usually have their first estrus (heat, or season) between six and ten months of age.

Socialization

- He's getting more sure of himself, maybe even cocky. But at around eight to nine months he undergoes a second fearful stage, when little negative experiences make a big impact on him. So continue to get him out and about, but with a watchful eye.

Behaviors

- He's still finding his place in the pack. Older dogs are now less tolerant of his transgressions. Keep an eye on them, but remember, the adult needs to lay down the rules to the youngster, and better now than later.
- He may try to push your limits, ignore your commands, and see what he can get away with. Deal with disobedience firmly, steering him toward more rewarding behaviors.

- Males that have not been castrated may start lifting their leg when they are eight to twelve months of age, and some do it inside the house. This is a hard habit to break and one you absolutely must try to correct early by watching him carefully and rushing him outside with a disapproving tone if you catch him in the act. A female may start to urinate more often as she comes into estrus, and especially, during estrus.
- He's reasoning more like an adult. Certain tests of memory and reasoning, such as "object permanence" (a test in which the dog detects that an object that was once there has been removed when he wasn't looking) show that dogs don't develop that ability until eight or nine months of age.

Care and Experiences
- It's time to update your puppy proofing once again.
- He's going to need somewhat more exercise than before. He needs to walk around the block, sniff all the neat smells, and see something new every day.
- If he regresses in his house training, you need to take a step back in your training. He may look like an adult, but remember, he's been on this earth less than a year.

Training
- He really should know the basics—sit, down, come, stay, heel—by now. If you haven't yet enrolled in a class, it's time you did so he can practice around others. If he is getting bored with the basics, add some tricks or some of the advanced exercises. It's easier for him to learn them now, while he's still in the learning mode.
- If you have special plans for your dog, such as therapy work or search and rescue, it's time to get with a group that can help you train him.

Play
- Try new, more complicated toys. Rotate his toys, so it seems to him he's getting new ones every few days.
- A lot of his play now centers on showing you how much faster, stronger, and smarter he is than you. You can play along, but make sure you win or are the one to say when the game is over.

Socialization

Think of socialization as puppy shots for the mind. If your puppy has lots of good experiences with children, and one day a child accidentally falls on her, chances are she will continue to like children. But if the child who fell on her was the first child she ever met, she might conclude that children are dangerous and develop a fear of them. Good experiences are like inoculations against future bad experiences.

This is why it's so vital to have as many guaranteed good experiences as possible before taking chances on having bad ones. The more you can control your dog's first encounters and outings, the better your chance of preventing him from forming bad associations before he's had a chance to form good ones.

Puppies start off life relatively fearless, but at about five weeks of age, they gradually start to get more cautious of new situations and people. Sometime after twelve weeks of age the fear response becomes the dominant one, making it difficult for the puppy to accept new situations he has never before experienced. This means that you have a deadline to meet, a deadline before which you need to make sure your puppy has experienced a wide range of people, places, and things to prepare him for the rest of his life.

When it comes to socialization, it's the quality, not quantity, that counts. Good intentions can too often lead to bad results if you overwhelm your pup. As with all things puppy, you need to introduce new experiences gradually, never pushing your puppy past the point that he's scared. Fear is easy to learn but hard to unlearn.

Your aim is to have your puppy comfortable around strange people, dogs, animals, places, and situations. Introduce him to different floorings, stairs, car rides, and things he'll be doing later in life.

Remember, you want introductions to go well, so it's a good idea if you have control over how meetings go. Ask friends to come over and to greet the puppy as strangers should, which means kneeling down and rubbing him under the chin or on the chest. You'll want your puppy to meet men, women, people in wheelchairs, people with canes, and people of all races, ages, and sizes.

Puppy Health and Nutrition

Puppy proofing means safeguarding your puppy not only on the outside, but on the inside as well, by means of parasite prevention, vaccinations, good nutrition, and good health practices.

Vaccinations

At one time vaccinations were a nonissue: it seemed the more the better was the mantra. Now veterinarians have adopted a more individualized approach to vaccination. The basic concepts of puppy vaccination remain the same, however. Without well-timed vaccinations your Dachshund can be vulnerable to deadly communicable diseases.

Your pup received his early immunity through his dam's colostrum during the first few days of nursing. That maternally derived immunity interferes with the ability of vaccinations to stimulate immunity, so vaccinations given while your pup still has that maternal immunity will be ineffective. But after several weeks that immunity begins to decrease. As his immunity falls, both the chances of a vaccination being effective and the chances of getting a communicable disease rise. The problem is that immunity diminishes at different times in different dogs. So starting at around eight weeks of age, a series of vaccinations is given to leave as little unprotected time as possible. During this time of uncertainty it's best not to take your pup around places where unvaccinated dogs may congregate. Deadly viruses, such as parvovirus, can remain in the soil for months after an infected dog has shed a virus in its feces there.

This doesn't mean you must load up on every vaccine available. Vaccinations are divided into core vaccines, which are advisable for all dogs, and noncore vaccines, which are advisable only for some dogs. Core vaccines are those for rabies, distemper, parainfluenza, parvovirus, and hepatitis (using the CAV-2 vaccine, not the CAV-1, which can cause adverse reactions and is still sold by some feed stores). Noncore vaccines include those for leptospirosis, bordetella, and Lyme disease. Your veterinarian can advise you if your dog's lifestyle and environment put him at risk for these diseases. Remember, more is not better!

A sample core vaccination protocol for puppies suggests giving a three-injection series at least three weeks apart, with each injection containing distemper, parvovirus, adenovirus 2 (CAV-2), and parainfluenza. A booster is given one year later, and then boosters (for core vaccines) are given every three years. Rabies should be given at sixteen weeks of age, with boosters at one- to three-year intervals according to state law.

Some proponents of natural rearing condemn vaccinations and refuse to use them. They use homeopathic nosodes instead, and point to the fact that their dogs don't get sick as proof that they work. However, their good fortune is probably the result of herd immunity; that is, as long as most other dogs are vaccinated, they probably never come in contact with the infectious agents. And no controlled study has ever supported the effectiveness of nosodes.

FYI: The Heartworm Cycle

- Mosquito feeds on infected dogs, ingesting pre-larval heartworms called microfilaria. The American Heartworm Society estimates that about 27 million dogs are not protected from heartworms. Heartworm cases are found in all 50 states, but are most prevalent within 150 miles of the Gulf and Atlantic coasts as far north as New Jersey, and along the Mississippi River region. In these areas almost half the dogs not on heartworm prevention are infected.
- Microfilaria mature into larvae and move to mosquito's mouthparts in 10 to 14 days.

- Mosquito bites an uninfected dog, injecting heartworm larvae into the dog's skin.
- Larvae burrow until they penetrate blood vessels and are carried to the heart and lungs. One dog may harbor as many as 250 heartworms, each up to a foot long, each living five to seven years. The worms initially cause inflammation of the surrounding arteries, and later, enlargement of the heart, congestive heart failure, and death.
- Adult heartworms mate and produce microfilaria that circulate in the dog's blood vessels.

De-worming

Your pup should have been checked and de-wormed if necessary before coming home with you. Most pups have worms at some point because some types of worms lie dormant and protected in the dam until hormonal changes caused by her pregnancy activate them and enable them to infect her puppies. Your pup can also pick up worms from the ground in places where dogs congregate. The best prevention at home is to clean up feces immediately. Most heartworm preventives also prevent many types of worms. Get your pup regular fecal checks for worms, but don't de-worm your pup unnecessarily. Avoid over-the-counter worm medications, which are neither as safe nor as effective as those available from your veterinarian.

CAUTION

If you see small, flat, white segments in your dog's stool, he may have tapeworms. Tapeworms are acquired when your pup eats a flea, so the best prevention is flea prevention. Tapeworms require special medication to get rid of them.

Heartworm Prevention

Heartworms can kill your dog. They are carried by mosquitoes, so if there is any chance of a single mosquito biting your Dachshund, he needs to be on heartworm preventive medication. Ask your veterinarian when he should

begin taking the medication, as it may vary according to your location. Dogs over six months of age should be checked for heartworms with a blood test before beginning heartworm prevention. The once-a-month preventive is safe, convenient, and effective. Treatment is available for heartworms, but it's far cheaper, easier, and safer to prevent them.

Spaying and Neutering

An intact (unspayed) female typically comes into estrus ("heat") twice a year, usually beginning at around eight months of age. Each heat lasts for about three weeks, during which she will have a bloody discharge that will ruin your furnishings or necessitate her being kept off them or wearing little britches. Her scent, which she will advertise by urinating more than usual, will call attention to your home to nearby males, and have them whining at her door. If you have an intact male of your own, he will drive you insane with his relentless panting, whining, shaking, and clawing. It will be the longest three weeks of your life.

You can stop the insanity by castrating (neutering) your male or spaying your female. The advantage to doing this before your dog reaches sexual maturity depends on the sex of the dog. When a male reaches sexual maturity, he starts to lift his leg when urinating to mark objects in his territory, which includes your furniture. He may also become more aggressive toward other dogs. The longer he does this, the more likely these behaviors are to persist after neutering.

The advantage to spaying a female before her first season is medical rather than behavioral. Spaying before her first heat season drastically reduces her chance of breast cancer in later life. Spaying before her second season helps, but not as much, and after that it has little benefit against breast cancer. Spaying at any time eliminates the possibility of pyometra, a potentially fatal infection of the uterus all too common in dogs.

The best age to castrate or spay is around five months. This gives your Dachshund a chance to grow, making surgery in tiny minis a little easier. Because it's not uncommon for small dogs, like minis, to have retained baby teeth alongside their permanent teeth, it also allows the veterinarian to remove such teeth if they don't want to fall out on their own by that age.

Puppy Food

Dachshund puppies eat just about anything, so it's up to you to make sure that what you put in their bowl is nutritious. Now is not the time to save money by buying the pressed husks and guts that passes for generic dog food. Feed a high-quality food made especially for puppies.

Your young puppy should be fed four times a day (five times for minis). Let him eat as much as he wants in about 15 minutes. From about four to six months of age, you can feed him either three or four times a day. From six to nine months of age, three times a day, and then gradually cut down to twice a day by the time he's twelve months old. You can add snacks, but don't let him get fat. If you see him packing on the baby fat, cut down the amount he eats per meal.

Hypoglycemia in Puppies

Low blood sugar, more technically known as hypoglycemia, can kill. It's an emergency condition related to feeding, seen mostly in small, young, stressed, or active dogs, including miniature Dachshund puppies.

Very small puppies can't store enough readily available glycogen (which is the form in which the body stores glucose), and when the glycogen runs out, the body breaks down fat for energy. But because puppies have very little fat on their bodies, this energy store is also quickly depleted. When that happens, the brain, which depends on glucose to function, starts having problems. The puppy may start to get weak and sleepy, perhaps wobbling and stumbling about if forced to move. If he still gets no glucose, he can have seizures, lose consciousness, and die.

To prevent hypoglycemia, never let your young miniature Dachshund puppy go more than four hours without eating during the day. If that's not possible, such as in the middle of the night, make sure he's warm and confined and quiet so he doesn't use much energy.

Next, make sure you're feeding foods that are fairly high in protein, fat, and complex carbohydrates. Complex carbs slow the breakdown of carbohydrates into sugars. This steady breakdown leads to more efficient use, rather than a roller-coaster ride of highs and lows. Avoid simple sugars such as sweets and semi-moist foods. However, keep some on hand, because they can be useful if your dog starts having signs of hypoglycemia.

If your Dachshund puppy is acting lethargic and uncoordinated, he may be hypoglycemic. If so, you need to get some simple sugars into him. Corn syrup is a good choice, but he probably won't swallow it. Rub it on his gums and the roof of his mouth. He may eat semi-moist foods, so try that. Don't put anything in his mouth that could choke him! Keep him warm and call your veterinarian. If you've gotten enough sugar in him, he should start showing signs of improvement while you're still on the phone—within a couple of minutes. He may still need to go to the clinic for intravenous glucose. Once he's better and can eat, give him a small, high-protein meal, such as meat baby food.

15 Biggest Mistakes New Dachshund Owners Make

1. **Not supervising enough.** Dachshund puppies are like infants that can squirm into holes, gnaw through wires, and run into roads as soon as you turn your back. Yet too many people let their Doxie pups have the run of the house or yard, perhaps locking them in a bathroom when they're gone. Unless your bathroom or kitchen can be totally puppy proofed, a better solution is to use a crate or small pen any time you can't be there to pay attention. It's not only the mischief your Dachshund can make on his own. It's the danger posed by others, especially outside. Dogs, coyotes, and even birds of prey have killed or carried off young Dachshund puppies, and dognappers may welcome the chance to grab an unwatched puppy.

2. **Inconsistent potty training.** Smaller dogs are notorious for being difficult to house train. Some of the reasons stem from their early experiences. Dogs that are raised in pens where they're forced to potty inside tend to be indiscriminant about where they go in later life. In fact, as adults, dogs tend to prefer using the same type of surface they pottied on as puppies. That means you need to decide where you want your puppy to potty as an adult and start using that same surface area when he's a puppy—even if it means hauling sod squares inside the house during bad weather. And you have to be consistent and watchful. You can't put off going to the potty area because the weather's bad or you're in a hurry. You can't decide to just let the puppy potty inside because it's easy to sop up off the tile. You can't make exceptions; you can't be inconsistent.

3. **Bringing home a puppy too young.** All dogs should stay with their dam and littermates until at least seven weeks of age for important canine socialization. In fact, in many states it's illegal to sell a puppy before the age of eight weeks.

4. **Not crate training.** At some point, whether during house training, a stay at the veterinary clinic, or forced crate-rest for a bad back, your Dachshund will need to be crated. Don't wait until he is already stressed to crate train. The time to start crate training is the day your puppy comes home. A dog that learns early to associate a crate with good things enjoys the crate as its own special den, often seeking it out when he's tired or has a special treat he wants to enjoy in private. If you wait until later, your dog is more likely to object, sentencing you to hours of barking and scratching, and subjecting the dog to unnecessary stress.

5. **Not crating in the car.** If you use a crate only one place, it should be in the car. Yet too many new owners want their Dachshund in their lap or on the seat beside them. Dogs can interfere with driving, distract the driver, and in an accident, be flung into the dashboard or out a broken window. Many dogs survive accidents only to be ejected from the car and flee in terror, never to be found.

6. **Too much trust.** Trust is the most insidious killer of puppies everywhere. Your puppy may seem like an angel who hangs on your every command, but all it takes is letting him off-lead one time near a road, and having a cat or other enticement appear for him to chase, and it's too late. Don't let your Dachshund run out the front door to hop in the car, because he may not stop and could end up in the road. It's not that hard to put the leash on, and it could save his life.

7. **Letting the dog answer the door with you.** Too many dogs rush outside the opened door, often into the road.

8. **Allowing the puppy to run in dog parks with larger dogs.** Even dogs with friendly intentions can easily injure a small dog.

9. **Not socializing.** Sometimes people forget that small dogs need to venture farther than their own backyard. They may not need to go hiking or jogging for physical exercise, but they need both socialization and mental stimulation. They need to meet new people and experience new situations. Good breeders will have started this socialization process before your puppy goes home with you, but you need to continue it.

10. **Allowing "cute" behaviors that won't always be cute.** Who can help but laugh at a tiny spitfire launching himself at your ankles, or barking at the giant dog on the sidewalk? Yes, it's cute now, but it won't be later. And some things, like barking at big dogs, might even get your dog killed. What's cute in a puppy can be obnoxious in an adult. It's far easier to teach good behavior than to correct a bad habit.

11. **Spoiling.** Half the fun of having a dog is being able to spoil it, but Dachshund owners have a tendency to go overboard! Think twice

before you designate yourself as your dog's personal valet. Just because your Doxie demands it doesn't mean he should get it. One of the most common ways miniature Dachshund owners spoil them is by carrying them everywhere. It's healthy for a puppy to run and jump and explore. Some minis become so used to being carried that they protest if they have to walk on their own. Another way of spoiling is to let your Dachshund get away with protesting when you're trying to groom him. Now is the time for your Dachshund to learn that he must put up with brushing, nail clipping, and tooth care.

12. **Ignoring Dachshund back issues.** Every Dachshund owner knows Dachshunds can have back problems. But too many don't do anything to prevent it. Roughhousing, holding the dog on his hind legs, letting him rush down stairs, and allowing him to become obese are all ways that could help bring on a back problem.

13. **Allowing strangers to pick up your Dachshund.** Many people don't know the proper way to pick up a dog, or get scared and simply let go. Dachshunds can be easily injured from a drop.

14. **Relying on Internet advice for medical and behavioral problems.** Some Internet advice is good, some isn't. By the time you figure out which is which, your Dachshund could be in serious trouble.

15. **Thinking a Dachshund will be a good breeding investment.** Too many things can go wrong, costing you a lot of money or even your Dachshund's life. Leave breeding dogs to people with experience.

CAUTION

How to Hold a Dachshund

It's important to pick up and hold any dog correctly, but especially a Dachshund. The main thing to remember is that you don't want to twist or stress his back unnaturally. Ideally, you should kneel down and slip one hand under his chest and rear, steadying him with the other hand around his forechest.

- Never just let him hang from his front legs or chest. Always support his loin and rear.
- Never just drop him to the ground. Always place him there.
- Never let him squirm from your arms. Always hold him securely.

Chapter Five

Living with a Dachshund

Dachshunds are dogs. This may come as news to their doting devotees, who think of them as demi-gods, or at very least, children in fur coats, but they are dogs, with all the endearing traits and frustrating habits that dogs love to show off.

Dachshunds Will Be Dachshunds

Understanding what makes your Dachshund tick will help you better appreciate the wolf in your house—even if those behaviors can get on your nerves!

Dachshunds Bark And sometimes, bark and bark and bark. Barking can be traced to the Dachshund's wolf ancestry. Although adult wolves seldom bark, juvenile wolves bark as an alarm signal when intruders enter their den territory. One popular theory of dog domestication speculates that domestic dogs are neotenized wolves, meaning dogs are like wolves in various stages of arrested development. Like young wolves, adult dogs remain comparatively trustful, playful, dependent, obedient—and barky. All these traits made them more readily integrated into human society. Barking in response to intruders was an especially valuable trait, a trait that is still valued in many dogs today. The barking of a hunting Dachshund helps alert the hunter to the dog's location, above ground or especially, below.

Barking and howling serve as auditory beacons, alerting the rest of the pack to the barker's location and drawing them all together. This is one reason a Dachshund left alone may bark and howl until the neighbors complain. Of course, some Dachshunds just bark for the entertainment value.

Don't get a Dachshund, or any dog, if you demand silence. But just because it's natural doesn't mean you have to let your Dachshund bark unchecked. See page 83 for ways of coping with excessive barking.

Dachshunds Dig Wild dogs dig for a number of reasons. They excavate dens in which to raise young, and they bury food for later consumption. They dig out prey. Digging is a natural and adaptive behavior. Young wolves

practice digging as part of their play repertoire, and since domestic dogs retain so many behaviors of young wolves, they include digging as part of their day's entertainment. Dachshunds were built as dirt excavators, and they definitely like to hone their skills to a fine art form. Don't get a Dachshund if the sight of a few holes marring your pristine yard makes you feel faint. But you can at least restrict it.

Dachshunds Chew A puppy explores with his mouth. Those exploratory talents include carrying, licking, grabbing, biting, and gnawing. These are skills an adult dog will need, so they are the skills a young dog will need to perfect. Unfortunately young house dogs may perfect their skills on your new shoes, antique furniture, and feather pillows. Even adults enjoy chewing, but usually, you can redirect it to more acceptable targets, such as chew toys and rawhides, by then.

Dachshunds Steal It's not that they are amoral kleptomaniacs. It's that dogs evolved as hunters and scavengers. Anything left unguarded was fair game and ended up in a smart dog's mouth. Fortunately, their limited reaching ability means most foods on your counter are safe, as long as you push them to the rear, but you do have to do your part. As your Dachshund matures, you can teach him that items on tables are yours, whether you're around to guard them or not. But don't put too much credence in those innocent eyes when you come back in and can't find that cookie you left on the coffee table.

Dachshunds Scavenge The dog's very first service to mankind was likely that of garbage man, disposing of wastes that would otherwise attract less desirable scavengers. And perhaps humans' first service to dogs was to inadvertently feed them at village dumpsites. Your Dachshund has no way of knowing that the miniature dumpsite you call the kitchen trash can is not just for him. Your best bet is to do like most resigned dog owners: Just keep the trash can under the sink.

Dachshunds Join Dogs are pack animals, and it's instinctive for them to join in whatever you or your family is doing. That means he's going to be unhappy shut in another room while you have company over, or shut home alone when you go out. Not only is he missing out on all the fun, but from an evolutionary viewpoint, being left alone is being put in danger. That's why many dogs, Dachshunds included, become anxious if left by themselves. They'll dig, chew, bark, and do whatever they can do to bring you back or to escape and find you. That doesn't mean your Dachshund can't learn to be alone. See page 84 for ways of dealing with separation anxiety.

Dachshunds Lick Licking is a natural dog behavior. Dogs lick one another as an appeasement gesture, often along with rolling over and giving the canine equivalent of "Uncle!" Puppies mostly use licking to elicit regurgitation from adults, particularly from their dam, around the time of weaning. Wild canids greet adults returning from hunting by licking at the adults' mouths in hopes of getting a meal. Domestic dogs continue this behavior into adulthood, licking at the mouth of dominant dogs and of humans. When your Dachshund licks at your face when you return home, he's not so much giving you sugar as acknowledging your leadership.

Dachshunds Sniff Dogs use sniffing as a way of getting to know each other, and they use it effectively to find out more about the people in their lives. Certain parts of human and canine bodies emit more information-laden odors than others, and these parts draw your dog's attention—as well as your embarrassment.

Dachshunds Guard Wild canids naturally protect their resources, whether food, territory, or offspring. By integrating domesticated dogs into the human family, they transferred their protectiveness to their new resources, the human's territory and family. Guarding was such a valuable trait that the tendency to guard has been accentuated in many domesticated breeds. Dachshunds are enthusiastic guardians of all things theirs, and they consider pretty much everything in sight to be theirs. But this possessive nature can be troublesome if your dog starts guarding things from you! See page 87 for advice when guarding goes overboard.

Dachshunds Bite Or can bite. Dogs hunt, fight, and protect themselves with their teeth. They perfect

Helpful Hints

It's not what you say, it's how you say it.

- Be consistent in the words you use and the way you say them. Dogs hear your words as sounds, not as vowels and consonants that mean the same thing no matter how they are said.
- Shouting or repeating won't help your dog understand a command. Teach commands in a normal voice, and say them just once.
- Use low-pitched sounds to make your dog stop doing something. They indicate power, aggression, and leadership, and are often used as threats.
- Use high-pitched sounds to encourage your dog to interact or play.
- Using long, drawn-out, monotone speech tends to slow or calm your dog.
- Using abrupt, low-pitched commands tends to stop your dog.
- Using a series of repeated short, high-pitched sounds that continue to rise in pitch tends to speed up a slow dog.

these skills through play-biting, which can often be too rough for our fragile human skin and clothes. Puppies learn from their playmates that when they play too rough, their playmate either gives them a warning rebuke or quits playing with them, so they learn to inhibit their bites. In the absence of playmates, that responsibility falls to you.

Breed Truths

Simply because Dachshunds have natural tendencies to act in certain ways we don't like doesn't mean we have to accept those behaviors as unchangeable. But it means we must understand that change won't always be easy.

Dachshunds Fight Dogs come from a culture of both cooperation and competition. A dog that exudes dominance will tend to remain unchallenged at the top of the pack and so fight less than one in the middle of the pack. Dogs that like to fight with other dogs may be naturally dominant animals that see other dogs as threats to their dominance, intruders on their territory, or rivals for their resources. If their dominance is well established and the pack order stable, they have less reason to prove a point, but otherwise it's difficult to tell a dove from a hawk. Of course, not every aggressive encounter results in a full-blown fight. Dogs communicate their aggressive intentions with growls, stares, rigid posturing, and direct confrontations, all of which give the other dog a chance to back down—usually.

Dachshunds Mount Dogs mount other dogs, and sometimes, your legs, for several reasons, not all of which are sexual. Young canids mount one another as part of play behavior, with the sex of the mounter or mountee inconsequential. This play behavior may play a similar role as play fighting and play hunting, preparing the pup for adult behaviors.

Dachshunds Roam Wild canids have a territory over which they regularly hunt. As hunters, Dachshunds are especially likely to roam and hunt. Unfortunately, unless you live on hundreds of acres, this means wandering into roads and neighbors' yards.

Dachshunds Hunt Dachshunds search out, follow, and kill prey. That's what they were bred to do. They'll chase cats, trail rabbits, and dispatch rodents given half a chance. It's your job not to give them that chance.

Talking to Your Dachshund

Communicating with your Dachshund means more than yelling his name to come. But dogs have a tough job trying to figure out what people

are trying to say sometimes. You can help by realizing how your actions and tones affect your dog's perception of what you're trying to communicate.

You may do some of these things without realizing it:

- Staring at a dog: Dogs consider an unwavering direct stare to be a threat. It can frighten or intimidate a dog.
- Bearing down on a dog: Dogs consider a stranger who strides right up to them to be threatening. The same is true for somebody who bends over them, a common occurrence for a little Dachshund. A better approach is to amble up and stop with your side facing a strange or fearful dog. Kneel down to his level instead of bending over him.
- Petting a dog on the head or back: It's human nature to pet dogs, but dogs consider being petted on the head or back to be a sign of dominance. So if your dog is already overly submissive, try scratching him under his chin or on his chest.
- Approaching a dog: Dogs consider somebody coming toward them to be a signal to walk in the same direction, and stay out of the way. But it's also how people tend to call dogs to them—and then they wonder why the dog turns around and trots away! You'll have better luck turning your back and walking the other way as you call.
- Hugging a dog: Hugging is not something dogs do naturally; the closest they come to it is mounting one another. So dogs have to learn to like being hugged, and even so, most aren't crazy about it.

Dealing with Behavior Problems

Nobody's perfect. Behavior problems are the most common complaint of dog owners and one of the most common reasons leading to dogs being surrendered to shelters or euthanized. And although you can't expect any dog to toe the line and never make trouble, you don't have to let such problems build until you feel there's no other choice. Preventing and dealing with behavior problems is just as important as giving your dog vaccinations or medical treatment should he be ill.

Excessive Barking

Dachshunds like to express themselves. Sometimes over and over. Dogs bark for different reasons, and understanding why your dog is barking is the first step to silencing him. But many Dachshunds bark simply because they are excited. Here's how to teach your dog a command to stop barking.

Helpful Hints

1. Don't yell at your dog to make him stop barking. He'll only think you are joining in the fun. If need be you can throw a can filled with coins or pebbles on the ground to distract him momentarily so he can be quiet enough to begin training.
2. Wait until he is quiet momentarily and then give him a treat. This may be easier if you have him sit and stay first.
3. Keep repeating this, gradually increasing how long he must be quiet before getting a treat.
4. Add a cue word, such as "Shh" as you start your timing. Eventually he learns that "Shh" means that if he is quiet, he will get a treat. Be calm and quiet yourself.

Not all barking is from being overly excited. Boredom barking occurs when the dog is left alone and has nothing else to do. Prevent it by bringing him inside or around the rest of the family. When he's isolated, give him interactive toys. Provide plenty of exercise so he's too tired to be bored.

When it comes to training dogs, everybody considers themselves experts. But when it comes to dealing with dog behavior problems, you want a real expert. For serious problems, a board-certified veterinary behaviorist is your best bet. Veterinary behaviorists are trained in diagnostics and treatment, and have the advantage of being able to recognize and treat organic problems such as brain tumors, epilepsy, and chemical imbalances that may be responsible for behavior problems. Your veterinarian can consult with one or refer you to one in your area (go to *www.veterinary behaviorists.org* for a listing).

Your obedience class instructor may also be a source of information. Like veterinarians, dog trainers vary widely in their level of behavioral training. Look for a trainer who is a member of the Association of Pet Dog Trainers (*www.apdt.com*) and certified through the Certification Council for Professional Dog Trainers (*www.ccpdt.org*).

Distress barking occurs when the dog is left alone and is distressed by his separation from you or others. This distress is often visible in other ways, such as drooling, panting, or trying to escape. It's futile to try to get him to stop barking unless you first treat for separation distress.

Separation Distress

Separation distress is a normal behavior of young dogs. Under natural circumstances, separation from the dam and littermates would be a gradual process, allowing the youngster to adjust. In domestic dogs, it's more often an abrupt process, often beginning when the puppy goes to its new home. The dog can become scared very easily when first left alone, and can quickly come to expect to feel afraid when left alone. When that happens, the situation builds on itself and works up to full-blown separation distress.

Signs of a dog with separation distress include whining, howling, barking, panting, drooling, pacing, and digging and chewing at doors and windows while you're gone. The dog may also have urinated and defecated on the floor or in the crate. Many people think the dog is spiting them, but dogs never destroy out of spite. The fact that your dog may look guilty when you come home usually stems from past experiences with what seems to him to be your irrational homecoming behavior. Here he is finally reunited with his loved one and you start acting crazy. He learns to act submissive when you return home, especially if the house just happens to be in shambles.

If you're still not convinced, set up a video camera and watch him while you're gone. You won't see a dog gleefully venting his anger on your home. You'll see a dog that is upset and perhaps near panicked. This is not a dog that needs to be punished; he's a dog that needs to be helped. Start with these steps:

Downplay Departures Minimize any cues that you're leaving. Don't turn the radio

or television on or off reliably, don't rattle keys, don't put your shoes on right before you leave, and don't have any big good-bye scenes.

Graduate Departures Leave for only short periods at first—maybe 30 seconds. Your goal is to return before your dog has a chance to get upset. Work up to longer times gradually, repeating each level several times before moving to a longer period of absence.

Use a Safety Cue When first training with short periods, give your dog a cue that says to him, "I'll be right back." You can spray some air freshener in the room, turn on a radio (if you don't usually have one on), or put down a special bed. You want him to associate the safety cue with feeling calm. If you must be gone longer than your dog can tolerate, don't give him the safety cue.

Downplay Returns Just as you downplayed your departure, return as though it was no big deal. That means no crazed reunions. Ignore your dog until he is calm, or better, give him a cue to sit or do some other behavior involving self-control, and then reward him for that.

Consider Anti-anxiety Aids Many dogs may not be calm enough in your absence to make much progress. The use of dog-appeasing pheromones, which are odors that mimic the calming scent of a lactating dam, has been shown to help some dogs. They are available from pet stores as a spray or room plug-in.

Tough cases may benefit from anti-anxiety drugs. As with all drug therapy, this is not something you decide to do on your own, but rather should be undertaken with the guidance of a veterinary behaviorist.

Fearful Behaviors

Even brave Dachshunds can be afraid. Common fears are fears of strange people, strange dogs, thunder, or gunshots. Helping your dog overcome his fears uses similar concepts no matter what the feared object or situation.

Expose Gradually Dog owners have a bad habit of coping with their dog's fears by immersing them in the fearful situation. For example, a dog that is afraid of people might be taken to a parade and held while everybody pets him. This only tends to make the fear worse for two reasons. First, because the dog has no control of the situation, it makes him feel more vulnerable and fearful. Dogs with a history of being able to exert control over their own lives tend to be more confident and more resistant to fear than dogs without such a history. Dogs can be given control by rewarding them for good behaviors that they initiate, for example, by letting them out of the crate for being quiet for one minute. Second, because of the intensity of the situation, the dog never has a chance to overcome his fear. In fact, it probably makes the situation worse.

You need to help your dog build his confidence and feeling of control when around a fear-provoking situation. You do this by combining several behavioral techniques, as follows:

Response Prevention Give your dog some control. Instead of holding him in place, or letting him drag you away from a scary person, for example, have him sit when the person is near, and as a reward for sitting, allow him to move farther away and sit again. Gradually extend how long he has to sit, or how close the person gets to be.

Gradual Desensitization Your goal is to start each session at a level that may cause some anxiety to your dog, but not so much that he is still fearful at that level at the end of the session. That may mean just letting the stranger walk within a few feet of him and ignoring him at first. Remember, your dog is learning to be calm. If he's still afraid at the end of a session, all you have taught him is how to be scared.

Counter-conditioning Getting your dog to do something incompatible with fear, such as relaxing, eating, playing, hunting, or walking, will help him associate good things and good feelings with the feared object. This is one reason taking your dog for a walk, or hunting, with another person is more helpful than meeting a stranger at a shopping center. You can have somebody visit while you massage your dog, or feed him in the presence of strangers.

Imitation Your dog won't be helped if he sees other dogs acting fearful, but he might be encouraged to join in if his best doggy friend is getting petted and eating treats from somebody else. Don't forget that your dog can cue off of you as well. Don't clutch him to you, pull on the leash, or coddle him when he acts fearful. Instead, if something startling happens, act as though it's funny; if a stranger appears, act jolly.

The same concepts apply whether your Dachshund is afraid of people, dogs, or loud noises. If you don't seem to be making progress, consult a veterinary behaviorist, who may prescribe anti-anxiety drugs to help in the initial phases of training.

Aggressive Behavior

Mark Twain said, "It's not the size of the dog in the fight; it's the size of the fight in the dog." Dachshunds take that quote to heart. They're tough when they have to be. Your job is to make sure they don't have to be.

Dogs bite for many reasons, including feeling threatened, guarding their territory or belongings, scrapping with other dogs, or challenging your authority. They can also nip through overzealous play.

Playful Biting is normal for puppies, but it still hurts and you don't want to encourage it. Instead, when your puppy grabs you, say, "Ouch! No!" and remove your hand. Substitute a toy. If the puppy continues, just stand there and ignore him. He'll soon learn that when he plays too rough, you don't want to play with him anymore.

Fearful Biting occurs when a dog is placed in a fight-or-flight situation and can't flee. It often occurs when a dog that's afraid of strangers is forced to allow a stranger to pet him. Unable to get away, the dog finally lashes out at the approaching

PERSONALITY POINTERS
Recognizing the Bite

Playful Biting	Fearful Biting	Aggressive Biting
Wagging tail	Tucked tail	Stiffly held tail
Bowing position	Crouched position	Stiff, tiptoe position
Running and bouncing	Slinking or cornered	Standing or charging
Barks and growls together	Whines and growls	Low growl, perhaps barks
Breathy exhale sounds	No such sounds	No such sounds
Mouthing	No mouthing	No mouthing
Eye contact	Looks away	Eye contact
Licks at you	Licks own lips	No licking
Lip corner pulled upward	Lip corner pulled back	Lip corner pulled forward
Repeated nips or grabs	Sudden bite, then retreat	Sudden hard bites

stranger. It can also occur when a dog has been punished severely and the owner swoops down to grab him, especially if the dog is cornered. Some dogs have found that warning growls or bites make the threatening person stop, which teaches the dog that such behavior is rewarding.

Treatment should center on helping the dog overcome his fears. Meanwhile, take the following precautions:

- Do not place a fear-aggressive dog in situations that could cause him to be afraid.
- Do not punish a fear-aggressive dog for his behavior. It only makes things worse because it verifies his fears.
- Do not force a fear-aggressive dog to face his fears, and do not corner or reach for him. These situations greatly increase the chance that he may bite, which in turn becomes self-perpetuating. Instead, call the dog to you and have him act calm or do a trick for a reward.
- Do not reassure or pet a fear-aggressive dog while he is acting inappropriately. This gives the dog the message that he is acting appropriately, which he is not.

Aggressive Biting can be from guarding territory or belongings, or from challenging you. Dachshunds tend to be territorial, and many don't hesitate to protect their home and yard from perceived intruders, even if they're invited guests.

Treat territorial aggression by removing the possibility that your dog will encounter somebody against whom to protect his territory. That means removing him from the fenced yard when passersby are expected, and from the front-door area when company is expected. He should be rewarded for sitting and staying when strangers arrive, and gradually moved closer to them. You can eventually have visitors bring the dog treats. Use of a head halter will give you better and more immediate control of your dog.

A dog that guards his food or toys can be dangerous around children, who often inadvertently stray too close. Unfortunately, some owners create a perfect war that never had to happen because of some idea that they will train their dog to allow food to be taken away by repeatedly taking the dog's food away. The only thing this accomplishes is to teach the dog that his food is indeed in danger. A better scheme is to convince the dog that hands near his food are bringers, not takers. As he is eating, drop special treats into his bowl. If you must take his bowl away, substitute another bowl with some treats in it.

CAUTION

How NOT to Correct an Aggressive Dachshund

You may have heard these methods suggested as a means of asserting your dominance over your dog. Do not use them. They have been shown to be ineffective, unsafe, and based on faulty interpretations of wolf pack behavior.

- Myth: "Scruff shakes are good corrections because they mimic the way a mother dog corrects her puppies." No! Mother dogs rarely, if ever, correct their pups by scruff shaking. Scruff shaking can lead to neck injuries, and is especially foolish in Dachshunds with their tendency to have back (and neck) problems.
- Myth: "Alpha rolls are good corrections because they mimic the way a dominant dog exerts its dominance over a subordinate dog." No! Dominant dogs exert most of their dominance simply by ignoring subordinates. When subordinates roll on their backs in front of dominant wolves or dogs, the subordinates do it themselves; they are never forced. Alpha rolls conducted by humans in attempts to subdue an already challenging dog often result in dog bites.

Dachshunds can be cocky, and some try to rule the roost, or at least, rule it in some situations. A dog may resist being uprooted from his resting place on the sofa, for example, and may growl to warn you off. Rather than entering into a power struggle with such a dog, prevent him from getting on the sofa in the first place. Or have him wear a short leash around the house, so you can pull him down without having a hands-on confrontation.

If your dog continues to challenge your authority, establish your position by remaining somewhat aloof and not allowing the dog to take liberties with

PERSONALITY POINTERS
Dachshund Body Language

Dachshund Mood	Friendly	Interested or Excited	Playful	Pleasure	Confidence
Stance	Advancing, relaxed	Active, stiff	Active, advancing	Relaxed	Facing squarely; standing sideways
Posture	Leaning forward	Leaning forward	Body lowered on front end only; shoulder or hip bump into another	Body upside down and rolling	Leaning forward; head held high, arched neck
Tail	Wagging	Horizontal or natural; wagging slowly and broadly	Wagging slowly and broadly	Wagging slowly and broadly or quickly and broadly	High
Ears	Forward or relaxed	Forward	Forward		Forward
Eyes		Dilated pupils	Dilated pupils, wide		Relaxed
Mouth	Relaxed		Open with lip corner pulled upward, often showing tongue		

Apprehension or Anxiety	Submission	Fear	Aggression	Dominance
Retreating	Retreating, freezing	Retreating	Advancing; facing squarely	Advancing; facing squarely
Body or head lowered	Leaning backward; body or head lowered (and/or twisted); body twisted upside down; head turned away	Leaning backward; body or head lowered; body twisted upside down	Leaning forward with stiff legged stance; paw, head, or neck placed on another's back	Leaning forward with stiff legged stance; paw, head, or neck placed on another's back; shoulder or hip bump into another
Tucked	Tucked and wagging; wagging quickly and broadly	Tucked	Raises, held stiffly and quivering	Raises, held stiffly and quivering
	Down	Back	Forward	Forward
Blinking rapidly	Turned away and squinting	Dilated pupils	Open wide and staring; dilated pupils	Open wide, staring
Licking lips; yawning; panting (may also indicate pain)	Licking the air toward you or another dog; front teeth showing with no signs of aggression; muzzle push	Slightly open with lip corner pulled back, all teeth showing	Agape with lip corner forward; face, nose, or lips wrinkled, teeth showing	

you such as pulling you around, jumping on you, or demanding food or petting when he feels like it. Be a leader by leading the dog in cooperative activities such as walks and training games. Don't fawn on him, even though you love him. Fawning is what subordinates do. You want your dog to fawn on you, and one way that might help bring him around is to ignore him for several days unless he earns your attention, even his food, by doing a simple trick, such as sitting, when you ask.

A Dachshund that bites can seriously injure a person, make you at risk for a lawsuit, and place him at risk for euthanasia. Consult a veterinary behaviorist if your Dachshund shows signs of aggression toward people.

Communicating with Your Dachshund

Scent   Like all dogs, Dachshunds use their sense of smell in social interactions. They get to know each other by first sniffing at each others genitals, anus, mouth corners, and ears, all areas that produce a good deal of scent. They may try to sniff people in these areas, too, so you may have to discourage them by pushing them away.

People don't tend to use scent much when communicating with each other or with dogs. However, if you're scared or stressed, your body produces adrenaline and also tends to sweat more, which may produce differences in your odor that your Dachshund can perceive. Dachshunds and humans tend to prefer different scents, but Dachshunds tolerate the bizarre human preference for shampoo and soap smells, although they generally don't like them. Some evidence exists that commercially available dog-appeasing pheromones, which are odors that mimic the calming scent of a lactating dam, may help alleviate stress in some dogs.

Hearing   Your Dachshund can hear mid-range noises about four times farther away than you can. He can hear high-pitched sounds you can't hear at any distance. The lowest-pitched sounds that dogs and people can hear are about the same, around 45 to 65 Hertz (Hz). However, people hear sounds of around 3000 Hz most easily (most people's voices are near that frequency), but dogs are most sensitive to higher pitched sounds of around 8000 Hz. The highest pitch that people can hear is 23,000 Hz; dogs can hear up to 45,000 Hz. That's why he can hear dog whistles and you can't. You don't have to shout at your dog, or even talk in a high-pitched voice, for him to hear you, although in an old dog with hearing loss, using a loud, low-pitched voice may help.

Vision   Dogs have color vision like people who are typical red-green colorblind; that is, they can tell blue from yellow but confuse reds, oranges, yellows, and greens. Even though dogs do see colors, they don't seem to pay a lot of attention to them. Dogs are also adept at discerning slight movements, which is why your Dachshund is able to read subtle changes in your facial expressions and body positions. They don't have great detail vision, so they can actually have difficulty recognizing you just from vision unless you move or talk or get close enough to scent. Domestic dogs are one of the few non-human animals that can interpret the meaning of a human pointing or looking at something. They are actually aware of your eye position and can use it to cue on where you have something hidden, for example. Dogs are very sensitive to being stared at. A strange dog can consider it a threat, although your own dog will probably be fine with it.

Taste Dachshunds seem like they'll eat anything! But even Dachshunds have their limits, and likes and dislikes. Compared to people, the greatest anatomical difference is the dog's lack of strong salt-specific taste buds. And while dogs enjoy sweets, they don't like saccharin, probably because it's been shown their taste buds respond more to the bitter aftertaste than they do to any sweet aspect.

Touch Puppies grow up needing to be touched by their dam and littermates, especially when sleeping, and this trait often remains throughout life. Dachshunds especially enjoy being touched and petted, and yours may shove his head under your hand to remind you of your duties. When adult dogs are petted, their heart and breathing rates decrease and they appear calmer. The best way to calm a dog through petting is to use deep muscle massage with long, firm strokes reaching from the head to the rear. Most dogs don't actually enjoy being hugged, because in dogdom, the hugger is usually showing his dominance in the form of mounting the huggee. But dogs do enjoy being held or allowed to snuggle close when resting. Most Dachshunds are part heat-seeking missile, and so won't pass up a chance to get as close as possible on a cold night.

Chapter Six

Health and Nutrition

You're the first line of defense when it comes to letting your Dachshund live life to its fullest—and longest. You need to safeguard him against accidents, monitor him for signs of illness, feed him a nutritious diet, and choose the other most important person for his health, his veterinarian.

Veterinary Care and Choices

Choosing a veterinarian entails more than flipping to the Yellow Pages and pointing. When making your decision, consider availability, emergency arrangements, facilities, costs, ability to communicate, interaction with your dog, and experience with Dachshunds, especially Dachshund back problems.

Most veterinarians in general practice can provide a wide range of services, but if your dog has a problem that eludes diagnosis or requires specialized treatment, let your veterinarian know if you are willing to be referred to a specialist. Such specialists can be found at veterinary schools and in private practices in larger cities.

Besides going to the veterinarian when he's sick, your Dachshund needs an annual wellness examination. Because dogs age faster than humans, a yearly physical in a dog is like a person having one only every five years or so, so some veterinarians even advocate twice-yearly exams.

Common Tests and Procedures

A wellness exam typically consists of examining the mouth, teeth, eyes, ears, and genitals, listening to the heart and lungs, feeling along the spine, pressing against the abdomen in order to feel internal organs, and very likely drawing blood for a heartworm test and getting a stool sample to check for worms or their eggs. Some veterinarians also draw a blood sample so they have baseline values for your dog to compare with later samples should he ever become sick.

BE PREPARED! Health Insurance

As veterinary medicine has become more sophisticated, it's also become more expensive, which has brought on pet health insurance. Pet health policies have annual premiums and offer different deductibles and coverage plans. The premiums depend in part on the dog's age and any preexisting conditions. Some plans cover routine care whereas others cover only illness or injury. Your own veterinarian may offer wellness packages.

Part of getting a Dachshund is preparing for an emergency situation, which too often may involve serious and expensive back problems. Another option besides insurance is to pay yourself the premiums you'd otherwise pay out, and keep them in a special savings account earmarked for veterinary care. And don't borrow from it!

If your Dachshund is sick, the veterinarian will perform many of these same exams, depending on the nature of the illness, and may also perform some specialized tests.

Some of the most common, and informative, tests your veterinarian may perform are blood tests, which include a complete blood count (CBC) and perhaps a serum chemistry profile. The CBC checks red and white blood cells, and can identify problems such as anemia, leukemia, and the presence of many infections. A serum chemistry profile provides information on how various organs are functioning. Within minutes the results can tell you if your dog feels bad because of kidney failure, liver disease, or pancreatitis,

FYI: Changes in Appearance or Behavior

These signs	may indicate (among other causes)
Lethargic, lying in a curled position	Fever, general illness, weakness
Irritability, restlessness	Pain
Clawing, panting, trembling, hiding	Pain, fear
Repeated stretching and bowing	Abdominal pain
Restlessness, retching, bowing	**Gut obstruction—EMERGENCY**
Pain when lifted	Back or neck pain, disk disease
Paralyzed or suddenly weak rear	**Disk disease—EMERGENCY**
Refusal to lie down	**Breathing problems, abdominal pain—EMERGENCY**
Refusal to put head down	Breathing problems, neck pain
Head-pressing, seizures	Neurological problems
Weakness, pale gums	Illness, internal bleeding, anemia
Dizziness, head tilt	Vestibular disease, ear infection
Loss of appetite	Illness, fever, kidney disease
Increased appetite	Cushing's, diabetes
Increased thirst (and urination)	Diabetes, kidney disease, Cushing's
Frequent, sudden, painful urination	Urinary tract infection
Difficult, painful urination; bloody urine	Kidney or bladder stones
Inability to urinate	**Blockage—EMERGENCY**
Regurgitating food right after eating	Esophageal/swallowing problem
Vomiting	Illness, poisoning, blockage, others
Coughing	Kennel cough, heart disease, tracheal collapse
Gagging (chronic)	Tracheal collapse, laryngeal paralysis, foreign body
Enlarged abdomen, progressive	Cushing's, pregnancy, pyometra, heart failure
Enlarged abdomen, sudden	**Bloat, internal bleeding—EMERGENCY**

Note that many other problems can cause these signs, and that you should always consult your veterinarian as soon as possible for a diagnosis and treatment.

FYI: Gum Color

Gums should be a deep pink, and if you press with your thumb, they should return to pink within two seconds after lifting your thumb (a longer time suggests a circulatory problem). Your Dachshund's gum color is the window to his blood, and should be one of the first things you check when you suspect illness.

Gum Color	Could Mean
Pale or white	Anemia, shock, internal bleeding
Bluish	Lack of oxygen, poor circulation
Bright red	Overheating, carbon monoxide poisoning
Brick red	High fever
Yellowish	Liver disease
Red splotches	Blood-clotting problem

for example, enabling the veterinarian to start treatment immediately. Blood is usually taken from a dog's legs, but because of their short legs, it's sometimes preferable to take the sample from the large vein in a Dachshund's neck. Either way it doesn't hurt him.

Other tests include ultrasound, radiographs, electrocardiogram, and even CAT scans.

Healthy Dachshund Checklist

Your Dachshund's health depends as much on you as it does his veterinarian. The veterinarian may use sophisticated tests to detect and diagnose health problems, but you have an even more powerful weapon: the knowledge of what's normal for your dog. Your Dachshund can tell you where it hurts, or if it hurts, but only if you know how to understand the signs.

Lethargy
Lethargy is the most common sign of illness. Possible causes include the following:

- Infection (check for fever)
- Anemia (check gum color)

- Circulatory problem (check pulse and gum color)
- Pain (check limbs, neck, back, mouth, eyes, ears, and abdomen for signs)
- Nausea
- Poisoning (check gum color and pupil reaction; look for vomiting or abdominal pain)
- Sudden vision loss
- Cancer
- Metabolic diseases

Temperature

A high temperature can make your dog feel sick, and could indicate that a trip to the veterinarian is needed. To take your Dachshund's temperature, lubricate a rectal thermometer and insert it about 2 inches (5 cm) into the dog's anus, leaving it there for about a minute. Normal is from 101 to 102°F (38.3 to 38.9°C). If the temperature is

- 103°F (39.4°C) or above, call your veterinarian for advice. Of itself, this is not usually an emergency but is a concern.
- 104°F (40°C) or above, go to your veterinarian. This is probably an emergency.
- 105°F or above is definitely an emergency. Try to cool your dog meanwhile

CAUTION

Diarrhea

Diarrhea can result from nervousness, a change in diet or water, food sensitivities, intestinal parasites, infections, poisoning, or many illnesses. It's not uncommon for dogs to have blood in their diarrhea, but diarrhea with lots of blood, or accompanied by vomiting, fever, or other symptoms of illness warrants a call to the veterinarian. Bright red blood indicates a source lower in the digestive tract, whereas dark, black, tarry stools indicate a source higher in the digestive tract. In most adult Dachshund cases the best treatment is to withhold food for 24 hours, and then feed rice and low-fat foods. In puppies, the possibility of hypoglycemia precludes this, so you must feed small low-fat meals. Ask your veterinarian about using anti-diarrhea medication.

by dampening his fur and placing him in front of a fan. Do not dunk him in icy water, which constricts surface vessels and traps the hot temperature at the body core.
- 98°F (36.6°C) or below, call your veterinarian for advice. Try to warm your dog.
- 97°F (36.1°C) or below, go to your veterinarian. Treat for hypothermia on the way by warming your dog with hot-water bottles, blankets, or your own body.

Dachshund Disorders

Every breed of dog has its own set of hereditary headaches when it comes to health problems. In some cases these problems became prevalent in the breed because one or more of the founding dogs happened to have the genes for that problem, and because of the closed gene pool that is a breed, those genes became widespread. In other cases the problem is a secondary effect of some aspect of the dog's desired conformation.

Dieting Your Dachshund

Dachshunds are supposed to be long and lean. When they're long and fat, it's hard on their backs, their joints, and their hearts. Gauge how much to feed your Dachshund by how much he eats and how much he weighs. You should be able to feel (but not see) the ribs slightly when you run your hands along the rib cage. An indication of a waistline should be visible both from above and from the side. There should be no dimple in front of the tail, nor fat roll on the withers.

Some disorders, such as heart disease, Cushing's disease, hypothyroidism, or the early stages of diabetes, can cause a dog to appear fat or potbellied. A dog in which only the abdomen is enlarged is especially suspect and should be examined by a veterinarian. A bloated belly in a puppy may signal internal parasites.

Most fat-looking Dachshunds are fat because they simply eat more calories than they burn. They need to lose weight, which you can achieve by feeding smaller portions of a lower-calorie food. Commercially available diet foods supply about 15 percent fewer calories

FYI: Dachshund Disorders

Disease	Symptom
Intervertebral Disk Disease	Ruptured spinal disks can cause paralysis (see pages 106–107)
Obesity	Excess weight causes other problems
Cushing's Disease	Hyperadrenocorticism (see page 153)
Diabetes	Causes excessive thirst, urination, other problems
Epilepsy	Repeated seizures
Acanthosos Nigricans	Black, thickened skin, beginning around armpits
Renal Hypoplasia	Underdeveloped kidneys
Bladder Stones	Mineral formations in urine
Cryptorchidism	Failure of one or both testicles to descend into scrotum
Von Willebrand's Disease	Blood-clotting disorder causes excessive bleeding
Microphthalmia	Abnormally small eye; a problem of double dapples
Progressive Retinal Atrophy	Progressive blindness (DNA test available)
Glaucoma	Increased pressure within eye, causing pain and blindness
Dry Eye	Insufficient tear production causes eye irritation, discharge
Pannus	Vascular tissue grows over cornea, obscuring vision
Entropion	Eyelid rolls inward, irritating eye
Gastric Dilatation Volvulus	"Bloat"; stomach twists and fills with gas; emergency
Brachgnathism	"Parrot mouth"; severe overbite
Panniculitis	Painful inflammation of skin's fat layer under the skin
Pemphigus	Autoimmune problem causing skin lesions
Demodicosis	Inability to fight mange caused by demodex mite
Pattern Baldness	Early hair loss starting in puppyhood
Elbow Dysplasia	Problems in elbow joint cause front-limb lameness
Patellar Luxation	Kneecaps slip out of position, causing rear-end lameness

CHECKLIST

The Home Checkup

Make several copies of this checklist and keep a record of your dog's home checkups. Check the following items that apply:

Weight: ☐ Increased? ☐ Decreased?

Mouth: ☐ Loose teeth? ☐ Painful? ☐ Dirty? ☐ Bad breath?

Gums: ☐ Swellings? ☐ Bleeding? ☐ Sores? ☐ Growths?

Gum Color: ☐ Pink (good) ☐ Bright red ☐ Bluish
☐ Whitish ☐ Red spots

Nose: ☐ Thick or colored discharge? ☐ Cracking?
☐ Pinched? ☐ Sores?

Eyes: ☐ Tearing? ☐ Mucus discharge? ☐ Dull surface?
☐ Squinting? ☐ Swelling? ☐ Redness?
☐ Unequal pupils? ☐ Pawing at eyes?

Ears: ☐ Bad smell? ☐ Redness? ☐ Abundant debris?
☐ Scabby ear tips? ☐ Head shaking? ☐ Head tilt?
☐ Ear scratching? ☐ Painfulness?

Legs: ☐ Asymmetrical bones or muscles? ☐ Lumps?
☐ Weakness? ☐ Limping?

Feet: ☐ Long or split nails? ☐ Cut pads?
☐ Swollen or misaligned toes?

Skin: ☐ Parasites? ☐ Black grains (flea dirt)? ☐ Hair loss?
☐ Scabs? ☐ Greasy patches? ☐ Bad odor?
☐ Lumps?

Abdomen: ☐ Bloated? ☐ Pendulous? ☐ Painful?

**Anal and
Genital Regions:** ☐ Swelling? ☐ Discharge? ☐ Redness?
☐ Bloody urine? ☐ Bloody or blackened diarrhea?
☐ Worms in stool or around anus? ☐ Scooting rear?
☐ Licking rear?

Tail: ☐ Limp?

If you answered "yes" to any of the above (not including pink gum color), contact your veterinarian for advice.

compared with standard foods. Protein levels should remain moderate to high to avoid muscle loss when dieting. It's hard to resist those pleading eyes when your Dachshund begs for a treat, but treats add up to lots of calories during the day. Substitute carrot sticks or rice cakes for fattening treats. Keep him away from where you prepare or eat human meals, and instead of feeding him leftovers when you're through eating, make it a habit to go for a walk. It will do you both good!

Dog food labels don't include calories, so you may need to calculate them yourself. Proteins and carbohydrates both have about 3.5 calories per gram, and fat has about 8.5 calories per gram. By multiplying 3.5 times the percentage of protein and carbohydrates listed in the analysis, and 8.5 times the percentage of fat, and then adding these products together, you will have the total number of calories per gram of a food.

Although thin Dachshunds are rare compared with fat ones, they do exist, especially when young. A thin adult should be checked by your veterinarian. Unexplained weight loss can be caused by heart disease, cancer, and any number of endocrine problems. If he checks out normal, you may be able to add pounds by feeding more meals of a higher-calorie food. Add canned food, ground beef, or a small amount of chicken fat. Heating the food will often increase its appeal. Add a late-night snack; many dogs seem to have their best appetites late at night.

FYI: AAFCO Requirements

Association of American Feed Control Officials (AAFCO) requirements for food descriptions, using beef as an example.

Label Description	% of Ingredient in Food, Excluding Water
Beef	>95% beef
Beef dinner/platter/entrée	25–95% beef
With/and beef	3–25% beef
Beef flavor	Recognizable by dog as beef

Decoding Dachshund Food

Buying dog food seems like it should be simple—that is, until you start listening to everybody's different idea of what's healthful and what's not. Of course, your Dachshund is one of your best judges. If he won't eat it, the food won't do him much good!

But you are interested in proper nutrition, and dogs don't always pick the most healthful foods, so you need to do your part and study the label. Here's a quick lesson in what to look for.

Description

Start with the front label, where the first thing you'll see is the name of the food and often, a general description. Words such as *stew*, or *in gel*, *aspic*, or *gravy* indicate the food contains more moisture, and although that moisture tends to make it tastier, it also means you're paying more for what you get. Words such as *dinner* or *entrée* or *with* or *flavored* also tell you something, because there are specific requirements for companies to use these terms.

Ingredient List

All ingredients in a food must be listed in order according to percentage weight, from highest to lowest. It's generally a good rule of thumb to look for foods in which the first several ingredients are mostly meat-based. Unfortunately, the ingredient list can be misleading.

By breaking down a less desirable ingredient into different forms, which are then listed separately, what is actually the predominant ingredient may instead look like several less important ingredients. For example, a food with the ingredients "chicken, wheat germ meal, wheat middlings, wheat bran, wheat flour" probably has wheat, not chicken, as its primary ingredient.

Then there's the moisture issue. Some ingredients, such as fresh meat, weigh more simply because of their moisture content, and may thus be placed higher in the ingredient list of a dry food than their dry matter justifies.

Regardless, stick with your rule of thumb: The more meat higher up in the ingredient list, the better.

CAUTION

What About Table Scraps?

A few table scraps won't hurt. But choose your scraps carefully. Avoid hunks of fat, which can bring on pancreatitis in susceptible dogs, and avoid the following human foods that are toxic to dogs:

- Onions cause a condition in which the red blood cells are destroyed.
- Chocolate contains theobromine, which can cause death in dogs.
- Macadamia nuts cause some dogs to get very ill; the cause isn't understood.
- Raisins and grapes can cause kidney failure and extreme sudden toxicity in some dogs.
- Sugar-free candy and gum containing the artificial sweetener xylitol can cause a potentially fatal drop in blood sugar and lead to liver failure.

Guaranteed Analysis

The guaranteed analysis represents the worst-case scenario of the minimal percentages of crude protein, crude fat, and maximal percentages of crude fiber and moisture.

Protein represents the building blocks of life, so in general, the more the better. Unfortunately, some protein is more digestible or has more needed amino acids than others, and the guaranteed analysis doesn't distinguish between them.

Fat percentage is handy in comparing the calories a food may contain, since fat has roughly double the calories of protein or carbohydrates. If fiber and moisture content are the same, a higher-fat-content food will have more calories.

Crude fiber is an estimate of how much of the food is indigestible. Higher levels are often found in weight-reducing diets.

You'll notice that dry foods seem jam packed with nutrition compared with wet foods. That's because wet foods have so much water in them that it makes their nutritive content look low. Here's a quick way to compare wet to dry food: Multiply the canned values by four. If they're "in gravy," multiply them by five.

10 **Questions** About Your Dachshund's Back ▬▬▬

 I always hear about Dachshunds with bad backs. What does that really mean? When you're speaking of back problems in Dachshunds, you're actually talking about a disorder called intervertebral disk disease (IVDD). Intervertebral disks are the cushions between each vertebrae of the spine. Each disk is made up of a tough outer shell that surrounds a gel-like inside. The disks are good at cushioning forces straight up and down the length of the back, but they're not as good at cushioning twisting or diagonal forces. Over time, the cumulative effect of these twisting or diagonal forces can cause the outer coating of a disk to rip, letting the gel squeeze out into the surrounding space and compress the spinal cord. When this happens, it can be painful, and it can also cause paralysis.

 Does the Dachshund's long back cause IVDD? Actually, it's not the long back that causes IVDD, and in fact, there's no correlation between back length and IVDD within Dachshunds. The real culprit is the gene that causes the Dachshund's short legs. This gene is for a type of dwarfism called chondrodystrophy, and in addition to causing short legs, it causes the gel in the disks to become calcified and hard, so it loses its elasticity. This makes the disk less able to work as a shock absorber and more prone to injury.

What are the chances that my Dachshund will develop IVDD? Unfortunately, about a quarter of all Dachshunds will develop IVDD to some extent during their lifetime. Most often, it first occurs between three and seven years of age.

 Is there some way I can lessen the chance of getting a Dachshund that will develop IVDD? The best way is to buy a puppy whose relatives have not been affected by IVDD. Breeders can X-ray their dogs any time after 18 months of age and get some prediction about whether that dog will develop IVDD. That's because dogs with calcification of the spinal disks at 18 months of age have a greater likelihood of eventually developing IVDD. A puppy having one parent with calcification has a higher chance of developing calcification and IVDD, and a puppy having both parents with calcification has an even higher chance.

Is there anything I can do to prevent IVDD? There are several things that may be helpful, but nothing that's guaranteed. First, don't let your Dachshund get fat. All that extra weight along the midsection places an unnatural strain on the vertebra and disks between them. Second, restrict overzealous jumping, especially anything that combines jumping with twisting. Some owners even discourage jumping off furniture, or going down stairs. Some people suggest that foods rich in soy lecithin, such as tofu, may be helpful in supporting the fatty sheath that surrounds the nerve cells of the spinal cord, but this has never been proved. Finally, crate train your Dachshund so that if he ever has a minor problem that could get better with crate rest, you won't have a problem confining him.

6 How do I know if my Dachshund has IVDD?

It depends on where it occurs. If it's in the neck, the dog may cry if you bump his head, or he may walk with his head down or back arched so he can keep his neck level. But most cases occur in the lower back. If it's just a slight herniation, the dog may walk stiffly and with an arched back. He may cry if you pick him up. As it gets worse, he may have a wobbly gait, perhaps dragging his toes. As it gets even worse, his hind legs will become paralyzed and won't even feel pain. Sometimes this happens gradually, but just as often, it appears to occur overnight.

7 What should I do if I think my Dachshund has IVDD?

Do not wait! The longer the time before treatment begins, the worse the prognosis. If your Dachshund wakes up paralyzed in the rear, you need to be on the phone with your veterinarian immediately and make plans to take your dog to a specialist that day. A completely paralyzed dog must have surgery within 48 hours or it will probably remain paralyzed.

8 Can IVDD be treated? Yes, although treatment is not always successful in severe cases. But more than half of dogs with mild to moderate IVDD will recover at least temporarily with corticosteroid drug therapy and absolute crate rest for several weeks. Note, however, that corticosteroid therapy is now considered controversial. About 50 to 80 percent of these dogs will have subsequent episodes. Dogs with severe or recurrent IVDD need surgery.

9 What about physical therapy? In mild cases, absolute crate rest is the best physical therapy. In cases that have required surgery, a program of gradually increasing exercise is best. Swimming is an excellent non-weight-bearing exercise. As he gets stronger, you can help support his hind legs in a sling so that he can use them just a bit.

10 Is it hard to care for a paralyzed Dachshund?

Sadly, many Dachshunds are permanently paralyzed from IVDD. These dogs can lead full lives, but they require extra care. If they are incontinent, they may need to wear absorbent diapers, and to have the urine washed off their legs or stomachs several times a day to prevent urine scald. They may need their bladders manually emptied several times a day to prevent urinary tract infection. Paralyzed dogs need extra-soft bedding to prevent bedsores. Carts are available that lift the hind legs in a sling, enabling the dog to get around, but the dog must be supervised.

Chapter Seven

Training and Activities

T he better behaved your Dachshund is, the more fun things you can do together. Some fun things require specialized training, but some require just the basics so that he can be well behaved in public.

Positively Training Your Dachshund

Modern training methods focus on rewards and positive associations rather than force and punishment. They produce happy, well-trained dogs that are eager to learn more. Most training classes now encourage the use of treats and toys as motivators and rewards.

The old school of dog training warned that if you started training your dog with treats, you would have to give your dog treats forever or he would quit working. How can you avoid spending the rest of your life as a walking treat dispenser? The best way is to still give treats sometimes, but to also give praise all the time. So you'll either give praise then treat, or praise alone.

When you first teach him something, you'll want to reward him every time he does it right. But once he knows it, you can cut back gradually, rewarding him only some of the times, but still praising every time. Like a slot machine, you should pay off at random times, so he's always wondering if the next time he does something will hit the jackpot.

If you train your dog before his regular mealtime, he'll work much better for food. In fact, instead of giving treats in addition to your dog's regular food, you can dole out his dinner bit by bit as rewards during training sessions. If you're in a hurry, just train for a few minutes, give a few rewards, and then give a jackpot of his entire meal.

Breed Needs

Training Equipment

Because these methods don't rely on force, you won't need to use a choke collar for training. A buckle collar will suffice. You will also want a six-foot leash (not chain!) and maybe a 20-foot light line.

Leash Walking

Leash training is often the pup's first introduction to formal training. Traditional trainers often advocate dragging the dog until he tires of fighting the leash, but there's no need for that. Here's what you do:

1. Place a buckle collar on the puppy and attach a leash. Give him a treat.
2. Lure him forward with the treat and give it to him. Keep luring him forward a little more and more as you walk slowly along with him at your side. Give him the treat every few steps.
3. If he wants to go in a different direction, or stops and rears, go ahead and walk in his direction a few steps before trying to lure him along again. If he absolutely refuses to move, carry him a short distance away and see if he'll walk back with you to someplace he wants to go.
4. As he gets better, then you can ignore him when he's stopping, being sure to reward as soon as he lets the leash go slack.
5. If he pulls ahead on the leash, dragging you, stop dead in your tracks. Don't pull back; just stand there. Only when he lets the leash go slack do you say "Good!" and reward or move forward. Practice this until he stops pulling as soon as you stop.
6. Next walk toward something he wants to reach. If he pulls, stop or even back up. The point is not to jerk your dog back, but to show him that pulling gets him there more slowly. When he stops pulling go toward the goal again. The goal is his reward, but the only way he can reach it is to stop pulling!

BE PREPARED! Training Tips

- Teach new behaviors in a quiet place away from distractions. Only when your dog knows the behavior very well should you gradually start practicing it in other places.

- Although you can train your Dachshund off leash when you are in a safe, enclosed area, train him on a leash when you are in an unfenced area.

- Don't train your dog when he's hot, tired, or has just eaten. You want him peppy and alert for class time!

- Don't train your dog if you're impatient or upset. You won't be able to hide your frustration, and your dog will be uneasy.

- No dog learns to do something perfectly at first. Always train in gradual steps. Give rewards for getting closer and closer to the final behavior. Be patient!

- Give your dog feedback ("Good!") instantly when he does what you want. The faster you mark the behavior like this, the easier it is for your dog to figure out what you like. Think of it as taking a picture of the moment you want to show to the dog and say, "Do this again!"

- Give a reward as soon as you can after saying "Good!"

- Don't forget to praise your dog as part of the reward!

- Don't start using a cue word ("Sit," "Down," and the like) until your dog knows the behavior.

- Say a cue word just once. Repeating it over and over won't help your dog learn it.

- Dogs learn better in short sessions. Train your Dachshund for only about 10 to 15 minutes at a time. Always quit while he's still having fun. You can train him several times a day if you want.

- Try to end your training sessions doing something your dog can do well. You want to end on a high note!

- Don't push your Dachshund too fast. His successes should far outweigh his failures. Just like you, dogs like to do things they're good at.

- Every step has to be repeated many, many times—we're talking hundreds of times to get it right sometimes! Be patient!

- Remember, your Dachshund didn't read the book! He will have his own way of doing things, and will progress at his own speed.

- Your Dachshund isn't dumb just because he can't catch on to a behavior. If he doesn't seem to get it, try a different behavior or a different way of teaching it. If he's smart enough to figure out how to find his food bowl, he's smart enough to learn a behavior. You just have to figure out how to talk to him in his language and make it worth his while.

Sit

Sitting is one of the easier commands you can teach your dog, and one of the handiest as well. If you teach it as one of your puppy's first tricks, he'll use it as his "go-to" trick when he wants something, and be inclined to sit as though to say "please."

Helpful Hints

Finding a Class Act

Ask your breeder, local veterinarians, groomers, pet supply stores, and rescue groups for suggestions about training classes, including puppy kindergarten classes. You can also contact local kennel clubs or obedience clubs (find them through *www.akc.com*), which may offer classes. Or go to the web site of the Association of Pet Dog Trainers (*www.apdt.org*) and see if any of those listed are near you.

You can teach a dog to sit in many ways, but one of the easiest is to lure him into sitting, as follows:

1. Hold a treat just above and behind the level of his eyes. If he bends his knees and points his nose up, mark the behavior and reward him. If instead he walks backward, you can practice with his rear end a few inches from a corner to prevent him from backing up.
2. Repeat this several times, each time moving the lure further back, until finally your dog is sitting reliably upon your command. Dachshunds don't have far to go!
3. Next, repeat but using only your hand without a treat to guide him. When he sits, give him a treat from your other hand.
4. Gradually abbreviate your hand movements until you are using only a small hand signal.
5. When he is sitting reliably, add a verbal cue, "Sit!" right before the hand signal. The verbal signal will come to predict the hand signal, and he will soon learn to sit to either.

Down

Having a Dachshund that will lie down quietly is a big help when you want him to stay in the room and impress your guests, if you take him to an outdoor café that allows dogs, or anytime you need him to stay out of the way. To teach your dog to lie down on command:

1. Place him on a raised surface and have him sit.
2. Show him a treat and move it forward and downward.
3. If his elbows touch the ground, say "Good!" and reward him. Even if he goes only part way, reward him. Then repeat, rewarding for going down farther. If he keeps trying to get up, you can cheat and place your hands over his shoulders to help guide him downward.
4. Next, repeat but without a treat in the hand you have been using to lure him. When he sits, give him a treat from your other hand.
5. Gradually abbreviate your hand movements until you are using only a small hand signal.

6. Add the verbal cue "Down" right before the hand signal.
7. Then teach him the down command from a standing position.

Stay

The Stay command is another that is essential for living with a Dachshund. It's a little bit more difficult for some dogs to learn compared with other exercises in which they get to do something. Because staying is essentially asking the dog to do nothing, it's taught by introducing the cue word "Stay" right from the start. Otherwise he wouldn't know the difference between a Sit or Down where you forgot to reward him and this new behavior of not moving. Here's how to teach your Dachshund to stay:

1. Cue your dog to sit. Say "Stay" and hold your palm in a "stop" signal in front of his face. Wait for a few seconds, then reward him and say, "OK!"
2. Tell him "Stay" and give him the stop signal, then pivot out in front of him. If your dog is having a problem getting the concept, you can have him sit on a raised surface or behind a small barrier so it's more difficult for him to move. Always be sure to reward him before you give him the "OK" signal.
3. Work up gradually to a longer duration. If he gets up, simply put him back in position and start over, decreasing the duration you expect of him.
4. Next work on moving to different positions around your dog, still remaining close to him. Move in front, to either side, and behind your dog, and gradually move farther away.

5. Introduce mild distractions, gradually working to greater ones. Remember, you want your dog to succeed!

6. Now you are ready to work on the stay in other locations. Be sure to keep him on lead for his safety when practicing in public areas. Eventually your dog should be steady just about anywhere.

7. Do the same thing with the Down position.

Come

Coming when called is the single most important behavior your Dachshund can learn. But he probably already comes to you when he wants to play or if you have some food. Always make sure you reward him for coming, even when you haven't called him. Your real goal, however, is to have him come when called. The best time to start is when your dog is still a puppy. Here's one way to teach a reliable come on command:

Helpful Hints

Always make coming to you rewarding. If you want your dog to come so you can give him a bath or put him to bed or do anything else he doesn't really like, go get him rather than call him. Practice calling him when outdoors or even around the house, giving him a reward, then letting him on his own again.

1. You will need a friend to help you, and a long hallway or other enclosed area. Have your helper hold your dog while you back away, showing your dog a treat or toy.

2. The dog should be pulling and whining to get to you and the reward. Once he is, your helper should release him so he can run to you. You can even turn and run away to increase your puppy's enthusiasm. Say "Good!" the moment he touches you, then quickly reward him.

3. Eventually you want to be able to touch his collar so you don't end up with a dog that dances around just outside your reach. To do that, wait until you touch or hold his collar before rewarding him.

4. Once he is running to you reliably, add the cue "Come!" just before your helper releases him. Practice this several times for many sessions.

5. Once he is coming on cue, let him meander around on his own. Call "Come" and reward him when he lets you touch his collar.

6. Finally, practice in lots of different places, gradually choosing places with more distractions. Keep your dog on a long light line for his safety.

Tricks

Sit and such are useful, but they're too easy! Your clever Dachshund will enjoy learning even more, so why not add a few tricks to his repertoire? Start with some of the classics, but then make up your own using the same concept of gradually shaping the behavior until he gets it right. Be sure to make it fun!

Shake Hands

Your Dachshund will need to know how to shake hands when he's at formal affairs.

1. Start with him sitting. Kneel facing him.
2. Reach for his right paw with your right hand. He may naturally give you his paw, but if he doesn't, use a treat to lure his head way to the left, so he's almost looking over his shoulder. That will make his right paw lift. Praise and reward him as soon as his paw goes up.
3. Keep repeating, until he starts lifting his paw on his own.
4. Add the cue words, "Shake hands," and give him your hand and reward him only when he shakes on cue.

Roll Over

Dachshund bodies were made for rolling over!

1. Start with him lying down. Show him a treat and move it over his back so he has to twist his head over his shoulder to see it. Give him the treat, and next time have him twist a little more before he gets it. Keep on asking for more and more, until he eventually ends up rolling over. You can help a bit at this point with a gentle nudge.
2. Once on his back, keep moving the treat to the opposite side so he has to finish the roll and end up back on his stomach before getting the treat.
3. Once he can do a complete roll easily, add the cue, "Roll over!" Only reward him for rolling over on cue. You can keep on adding roll after roll. Just don't get him too dizzy to do the next trick!

Speak

Dachshunds are never shy about speaking their minds, but teaching your Dachshund to speak on cue is not only a fun trick, but a way to teach him the difference between desirable barking and undesirable barking.

1. First, figure out what makes him bark. The best situation is if he barks at you to urge you to give him a treat. Once he barks, say "Good!" and reward him.
2. Introduce the cue word ("Speak!") quickly for this trick. You don't want to reward him for speaking out of turn!
3. Once you've introduced the cue word, never reward him for speaking on his own.

The Dachshund Good Citizen

You'll probably spend a good deal of time with your Dachshund in public. As such, you and he will represent Dachshunds and their owners to a wide segment of the population. If your dog barks and lunges, or throws himself on everyone he meets, he will give the breed a bad reputation, and just as important, the two of you will miss out on a lot of opportunities you could have shared because you'll have to leave him at home.

The AKC offers a simple test where your dog can demonstrate his ability to behave in public and earn a Canine Good Citizenship title. To earn the title he will be asked to do the following:

Helpful Hints

How to Earn Your Dachshund's CGC

To find an upcoming CGC test, or learn more about it, go to *www.akc.org/events/cgc/*

- Accept a friendly stranger without acting shy or resentful, or breaking position to approach; sitting politely for petting and allowing the stranger to examine his ears, feet, and coat, and to brush him.
- Walk politely on a loose leash, turning and stopping with you, walking through a group of at least three other people without jumping on them, pulling, or acting overly exuberant, shy, or resentful. He need not be perfectly aligned with you, but he shouldn't be pulling.
- Sit and lie down on command (you can gently guide him into position) and then stay as you walk 20 feet away and back.
- Stay and then come to you when called from ten feet away.
- Behave politely to another dog and handler team, showing only casual interest in them.
- React calmly to distractions such as a dropped chair or passing jogger without panicking, barking, or acting aggressively.
- Remain calm when held by a stranger while you're out of sight for 3 minutes.
- Refrain from eliminating, growling, snapping, biting, or attempting to attack a person or dog throughout the evaluation.

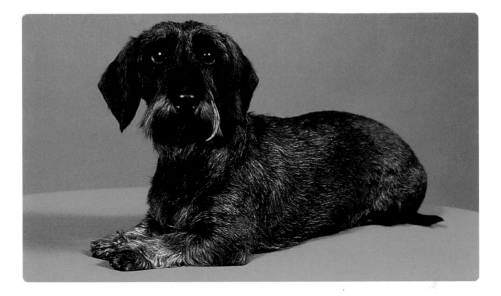

All the tests are done on leash; a long line is provided for the Stay and Recall exercises. The Canine Good Citizenship title is one of the most important ones your Dachshund can earn.

Therapy Dachshunds

Dachshunds are medicine for the soul. They lift your spirits, make you laugh, and shower you with love. Many Dachshunds share that love with people who aren't able to have a dog. They visit people in nursing homes, children in hospitals, and homebound neighbors who relish the chance to interact with a dog.

Therapy-dog training entails extensive socialization to people, places, and situations. Therapy Dachshunds that visit hospitals or nursing homes must be comfortable around wheelchairs, walkers, and medical equipment. They must be accustomed to not only the sights and sounds of hospitals and nursing homes, but also the odors and slick floors. All therapy dogs must have basic obedience lessons and be able to perform their jobs in the face of many distractions. They should naturally love meeting new people in new places. It's not a job for an introvert; in fact, such a dog could hurt the feelings of a patient who might conclude he or she had done something

Helpful Hints

How to Get Certified

Several certifying organizations exist, but the two largest ones in North America are Therapy Dogs International (TDI) and the Delta Society.

Therapy Dogs International
www.tdi-dog.org

The Delta Society
www.deltasociety.org

wrong. However, some dogs do better with children, and some with seniors. Some like noisy situations, others like quiet ones; some like to snuggle, and others like to perform. Finding a particular dog's talents is an important part of preparation.

Therapy dogs and their owners must pass a test that includes obedience, the ability to leave food, toys, and medications alone when working, the ability to tolerate being petted all over their bodies, and the ability to be quiet when asked. Maybe the worst part of therapy-dog preparation is learning to tolerate a bath before visits! Not only is it nicer to snuggle with a clean dog, but many therapy dogs visit people with fragile immune systems. Finally, therapy-dog owners must know what to do in unexpected situations. They must protect their Dachshunds from being hugged too hard, dropped, grabbed, or allowed to jump off a lap onto a slippery floor.

Most therapy-dog certification requires the dog to first pass the Canine Good Citizen test (see page 116). They must then pass additional requirements, such as being around wheelchairs and walkers without getting upset; leaving food alone; remaining confident around people who shuffle, cough, or even shout; remaining calm when left alone with a trusted person; and being willing to greet a stranger. Dogs must be at least one year of age.

Hitting the Road

It's the magic word guaranteed to transform your Dachshund into a whirling bundle of manic weiner dog: "Wannagoforaride?"

Dachshunds are great copilots, calm enough to travel quietly, active enough to enjoy excursions to see the sights, and small enough that you don't have to plan your next car purchase around them. But taking any dog on a car trip takes some planning. You'll need to find motels that allow dogs, and you'll need to make plans for keeping him safe and comfortable when you stop to eat, shop, or sightsee.

Helpful Hints

Online Travel Resources

www.1clickpethotels.com

www.aaa.com

www.canineauto.com

www.dogfriendly.com

www.doggonefun.com

www.fidofriendly.com

www.petsonthego.com

www.takeyourpet.com

www.travelpet.com

www.travelpets.com

Motel Manners

Fortunately, many motels still leave their doors open to well-mannered pets, but their numbers are decreasing as more dog owners abuse the privilege. To keep pets welcome, be sure you follow these rules:

- Bring his crate, or at least his own dog bed, in the room with you. If he gets on the bed, bring a sheet or roll down the bedspread so he doesn't get hair on it.
- Never leave your dog unattended in the room. He could feel deserted and try to dig his way out the door, or simply bark the whole time.
- If he has an accident on the carpet, don't try to hide it. Clean what you can and tell the management. Leave a big tip for housecleaning.
- Don't wash food bowls in the sink. The food clogs the drain.
- Clean up any dog poop your dog deposits.
- Be considerate of others. Don't let him bark!

Car Travel

You'll be wearing a seat belt while you drive; your Dachshund should have the equivalent, a crate that's secured to the car. Otherwise, if you slam on the brakes or have an accident, your Dachshund can become a flying missile, striking you or the dashboard, or being ejected from the car. As an extra safety measure, place emergency information on the side of the crate that says something like "In case of emergency, take this dog to a veterinarian, then contact the following people [and list their contact information]. Payment of all expenses incurred is guaranteed." (Include

a signed consent form, or the name of an emergency person who can provide a credit card number.) Include information about any medications or health problems your dog may have. You may not always be able to speak for your dog after an accident.

Of course, your dog should be wearing identification as well, and not with just your home phone. If you're on vacation, add a contact number of somebody back home or where you can be reached.

CAUTION

Beware of Parked Cars

Despite all the warnings about leaving dogs in cars in summer heat, many dogs die every year from just that. Studies show that the temperature inside cars can heat to lethal temperatures within 30 minutes even if the weather outside is relatively cool. Regardless of outside air temperature, cars heat up at a similar rate—gaining 80 percent of their final temperature within 30 minutes. Cars that start at a comfortable 72°F (22°C), for example, soar to a deadly 117°F (47°C) after 60 minutes in the sun. Cracking the windows scarcely affects the temperature inside.

Walking and Hiking

Dachshunds like to get out on the town, whether strutting along Rodeo Drive or galloping down a wilderness trail. Your Dachshund won't be content to let you lounge in front of the television, so get ready to get out and about.

If you're walking around the block, consider using a retractable leash and a harness. Know your area, and don't let your dog close enough to the road that he could run in front of a car, and don't let him relieve himself in anybody's yard. In fact, bring a plastic bag so you can clean up any mess he deposits.

If you have more ambitious hiking goals, you'll need to work up to longer distances. Remember, Dachshunds have short legs, so you may want to bring a papoose-like dog bag that you can carry him in should he get tired.

Winter Warnings Walking in a winter wonderland takes on a new meaning when that walk includes a Dachshund burrowing under the snow. Even old Dachshunds seem to get a spark of excitement from the frost on their breath. But you need to take some precautions amidst all this excitement.

For one thing, because Dachshunds are so low, they can become chilled from snow on the ground or all over their bodies very easily. They can get frostbite or become hypothermic, and even die, if left out in frigid temperatures. Several factors affect how well a dog can deal with cold temperatures.

- **Hair:** Even longhaired Dachshunds don't have particularly thick coats, nor do wire and certainly not smooth Dachshunds. The long outer coat may repel water, but doesn't add that much resistance to cold.
- **Size:** Dogs amass body heat according to volume, and lose it according to surface area. The Dachshund's long tubular body loses more body heat than the round body of another dog. On the plus side, it doesn't lose much heat through its legs!
- **Health:** Dogs with poor health or nutrition lack the resistance that healthy dogs have. They may also lack body fat, which is a valuable source of insulation.
- **Age:** Very young or very old dogs are very likely to lack appropriate fat for insulation, and tend to be more prone to hypothermia.

Remember, even the most macho Dachshund won't mind wearing a sweater or coat on cold days!

Snow and ice can form into little balls inside a dog's paws, so you need to check them regularly. Trimming long hair from between the toes can help prevent this. Salt and de-icing chemicals irritate paws, and can be toxic if your dog licks them off his paws. You can prevent problems by having him wear booties, but Dachshunds often draw the line at that fashion statement.

Hot Dogs Dachshunds handle heat better than many breeds, but not as well as humans. In hot weather, schedule your walks early, before the pavement gets hot, or very late, after it's cooled. Don't take your dog for long hikes, and don't leave him in the yard without shade, water, and ventilation. Dogs, especially light-skinned dogs, can get sunburn and melanoma. If your dog likes to sun-worship, rub a sun-block on his belly and the top of his nose, the most common sites.

Consider adding a shallow wading pool to his yard accessories. If you have a real swimming pool, take the time to teach him to swim and to find where the pool steps are. If there are no steps, you can buy a floating platform for him to climb up on. Dachshunds are not built for swimming, and should never be left unsupervised around pools.

When traveling alone, be sure you have a way to keep your dog cool should you have to run inside a rest stop. This may mean bringing an extra set of keys so you can keep your car, and air-conditioning, running, or locking him in a crate, locking the crate to the car, and leaving a window open along with a battery-operated fan. Ice packs, or better, one of the cooling pads made for dogs using water-retaining gel pellets, can also help keep things cool. But don't rely on any such measures for any longer than it takes you to hurry to the bathroom and back.

Outdoor Activities

Hunting

Dachshunds were bred as versatile hunters, and anyone who has lived with a Dachshund around wildlife, from bugs to badgers, knows the Dachshund's love of the hunt. Sometimes this gets him into trouble, as he follows his nose far afield, oblivious to danger. More often, it occupies his days and probably, dreams, as he schemes to capture one of those squirrels outside his window.

Dachshunds of all sizes can partake in rabbit hunting, but smaller Dachshunds are the choice for going in after woodchuck. They can locate a den and enter the woodchuck's burrow to either bolt it or confront it. If you plan to use your Dachshund to hunt woodchuck, or for any sport that may have him going underground, you must have him wear a radio locator collar. Otherwise some Dachshunds have been known to stay underground for

ACTIVITIES Hunting Titles

The American Working Terrier Association issues the Working Certificate (WC) for Dachshunds that perform successfully on badger, woodchuck, raccoon, or aggressive opossum. A successful dog must locate his quarry and enter its den, and then bark or otherwise alert the hunter that he's found the animal. He must then either bolt it or pull it from the den, or stay with it until the hunter dogs it out.

The AWTA awards the Hunting Certificate to Dachshunds that are regularly used to hunt game such as rabbits, squirrels, opossums, rats, raccoons, and muskrats, and even for flushing or retrieving upland birds over a full hunting season.

The North American Teckel Club offers a variety of hunting tests that encompass following blood trails, flushing rabbits, locating and trailing small game, and locating and either bolting or baying underground quarry.

days, reluctant to leave a cornered animal. And some have become trapped underground. With a radio locator, you can call down the hole. But bring a shovel, because you still may have to dig him out.

Follow Your Nose

Anyone who's tried to hide treats from a nosey Dachshund knows that the Dachshund's nose knows all. It's jam packed with olfactory cells, about 125 million in a typical standard Dachshund, compared with 6 million in your nose. But before your Dachshund sticks his nose too far up in the air, remind him that the German Shepherd has about 220 million. Still, 125 million is plenty to track down anything he sets his mind to following.

ACTIVITIES Tracking Titles

If your Dachshund has a knack for following a track, he can earn various tracking titles offered by the AKC.

Title	Track Length	Turns	Track Age	Surface
Tracking Dog (TD)	440–500 yards	3–5	0.5–2 hours	natural
Tracking Dog Excellent (TDX)	800–1000 yards	5–7	3–5 hours	varied natural
Variable Surface (VST)	600–800 yards	4–8	3–5 hours	varied natural and man-made

A Champion Tracker (CT) title is earned by a dog that has earned the TD, TDX, and VST titles.

For more information visit *www.akc.org/events/tracking*.

You can play scent games at home. Rub your scent on a stick and throw it a few times, closer and closer to other sticks. At first let your dog see it land, and then have him search for it without seeing exactly where it went. He'll be able to bring you the same stick you tossed, even from a forest of sticks.

Breed Truths

"Spurlant" Dachshunds

Baying, or giving tongue, is considered desirable for a hunting Dachshund because it lets the person know where their dog is, and also lets the hunter gauge what sort of activity is going on. It's easier to chase after a baying dog than a silent one, and more fun, too. A Dachshund with the tendency to bay on the trail is said to be spurlant, which in German means "loud on the trail." It's a desirable, but not common, trait in Dachshunds.

Another game you can play inside is to hide dog treats around the room. At first let him watch you hide them, and don't hide them too well. As he learns the ropes, make him wait in the next room as you hide them, and stick them under furniture or in remote areas. This is a fun way for a Dachshund to work for his supper, which is especially good for dogs that eat too fast or too much. Just hide kibble instead of treats.

You can teach him to track with just a little more work. One way is to find an area where you haven't walked over recently, and without your dog, walk a short distance, dropping treats along the trail. Then go get him and let him follow from treat to treat. Then repeat it in another fresh area, dropping the treats slightly farther apart. Eventually he'll figure out he can find the treats by following your scent trails, and you can leave a cache of treat treasure at the end of the trail.

You can also simply hide from him, assuming he wants to find you! This works best if you have a helper hold him while you go hide, walking over fresh ground and hiding in a bush or other covered area. Greet him with lots of praise and a few treats!

Field of Dreams (and Rabbits)

Although the Dachshund's fame is as a badger dog, they're just as adept as rabbit dogs, and Dachshund field trials allow them to track and locate rabbits. Fortunately, they are not expected to go into a rabbit hole nor kill the rabbit. In fact, if a rabbit actually appears, the judges will often order the dogs to be held.

Dachshund field trials are held in large fenced areas. A line of people walk across an area, flushing a rabbit and noting its location. Then two Dachshunds are brought to the spot and encouraged by their handlers to find the scent. Once the dog has found the scent, the handler releases him and can no longer talk to him. The two Dachshunds should follow along the rabbit's scent trail, followed in turn by the judges, then handlers. The dogs are judged in relation to each other on their prowess in finding the trail, their persistence in

Helpful Hints

Follow Your Nose

AKC Earthdog Information: *www.akc.org/events/earthdog*

AKC Tracking Information: *www.akc.org/events/tracking*

AKC Field Trial Information: *www.akc.org/events/field_trials/dachshunds*

American Working Terrier Association: *www.dirt-dog.com*

Born to Track: *www.born-to-track.com*

Dallas–Fort Worth Dachshund Club field trial pages: *www.dfwdachshund.com*

Deer Search: *www.deersearch.org*

JGV-USA: *www.jgv-usa.org*

North American Teckel Club: *www.teckelclub.org*

ACTIVITIES Earthdog Test Levels

Test	Entrance	Tunnel Length	Turns
AKC			
Introduction to Quarry	10 ft from release	10 ft	1
Junior Earthdog	10 ft from release	30 ft	3
Senior Earthdog	20 ft from release, steep, partially hidden	30 ft	3
Master Earthdog	100 ft from release, partially hidden, blocked	30 ft	3
AWTA			
Novice	10 ft from release	10 ft	1
Open	10 ft from release	30 ft	3

*Certificate of Gameness

following it, the degree to which they bay, and whether they flush the rabbit. The winners of each pair, as well as other impressive competitors, are brought back for a second series of judging.

Dachshunds placing first through fourth earn from one-quarter (fourth place) to one (first place) point for every dog competing in that stake. These points count toward the 35 points needed to become a Field Champion.

Get Ready! You can't just take your Dachshund to a field trial and expect him to make a good showing. Even though training for Dachshund trials is far less rigorous than training for many field sports, it still involves some preparation. Your dog should be socialized to people (at least two handlers and two judges will be following him on the trail) and to other dogs (he'll be off leash with another Dachshund). He'll need to be familiar with the sort of terrain the trail is set in, which means taking him for walks in the woods and fields. He'll need to be somewhat obedient, as you'll need to catch him when the judges tell you to pick him up. He should know to be quiet on command, because barking dogs are distracting to dogs that are competing. He should also not drag you around on the leash while you're trying to walk him, as it can become very tiring for both of you.

Hardships	Time Limit	Rat Working	Title
—	60 sec	30 sec	—
—	30 sec	60 sec	JE
False entrance, false exit, false den. Dog must exit how it came in.	90 sec	90 sec	SE
as in SE	60 sec to find tunnel	90 sec	ME
2 dogs take turn	90 sec in tunnel		
—	60 sec	30 sec	
—	30 sec	60 sec	CG*

Of course, your Dachshund should also be versed in trailing rabbit scent. You can start by buying some rabbit scent at a sporting-goods store. Apply some to a rag or rabbit skin and drag it in a straight line. When he finds the lure at the end, let him play tug with it. Make a big deal over his finding it. Then add a turn, so the trail is a little harder. You're also training yourself at this time. How does he act when he's caught the scent? How does he act when he's still unsure? The better you know your dog, the better able you can read him at a trial and know when he's caught the scent and is ready to be let loose.

For the next step you'll need real rabbits. The best way to find them is to go out at night with a flashlight. Note where a rabbit was before it hops away, but don't let your Dachshund see where it went. You want him to have to use his nose to find it. Be sure to keep him on a long leash. When you know he's following the trail, give him lots of praise, especially if he can lead you to a burrow.

Deer Trailing

In some European countries, hunters are required to use dogs to track down wounded game. Dachshunds have proven themselves so adept at this humane endeavor that they are the preferred breed. Wirehaired Dachshunds from European lines are most sought after for this activity, called blood trailing. Unfortunately, only a few states in America allow dogs to be used for this purpose.

New York is one state that allows blood trailing, and Deer Search, an organization centered there, receives 400 to 500 calls each year asking for

ACTIVITIES Rally Signs and Titles

Class	Title	Leash	# of Signs	Stationary Exercises	Jumps	Exercises
Novice	RN	on	10–15	No more than 5	0	Basic list
Advanced	RA	off	12–17	No more than 7	1	Novice plus pivots, call front, stand
Excellent	RE	off	15–20	No more than 7	1–2	Advanced plus reverse, moving stand, honor

their help in locating wounded deer. Many of the trails are 12 hours old and crossed by other trails; they often backtrack or wind through thickets, across roads, and into water. The Deer Search breed of choice? The Dachshund.

Dachshunds seem to do well at blood trailing because they tend to track at a slower pace and be less tempted to follow fresher cross trails of other animals. Their small size makes them easy to transport and more able to crawl into dense thickets, but it is a liability in really rough terrain, or in snake country. When the dogs find a wounded deer, they are not to attack or corner it.

In a blood-tracking competition, a leashed dog follows a track of aged deer blood. Deer Search, the North American Teckel Club, and JGV-USA all conduct blood-tracking trials.

Fun Facts

Dachshund ME Titlists

Don't feel out of place just because your Dachshund is the only hound at a terrier event. Feel cocky—because four of the first five dogs of any breed to earn the ME title were Dachshunds, not terriers!

Dachshunds Underground

Dachshunds were built to squeeze into dark, narrow burrows in pursuit of their quarry. As much as most Dachshunds would love to do just that, most Dachshund owners are understandably not so crazy about their dog disappearing down a hole to confront some unknown adversary.

Earthdog trials allow both of you to be content. Most earthdog trials are designed for terriers, but Dachshunds have no trouble substituting a rat for a badger. No animals are hurt during such trials, because they are safely ensconced in a cage underground. The dog is released near the tunnel entrance and expected to enter the tunnel and follow it to the rat, and then

mark the find by scratching, barking, or otherwise letting you know. Tests are offered by both the AKC and the American Working Terrier Association (AWTA), with different levels offered for dogs of different experience.

Mind Games

Hunting and outdoor activities may not be your idea of a nice outing with your Dachshund. Don't worry, plenty of other activities exist for the two of you, many of which spotlight how your Dachshund is obviously long on brains.

Rally

One of the most popular obedience-oriented sports is AKC Rally Obedience, in which you and your Dachshund go through a course consisting of 10 to 20 signs, each of which has instructions telling you which exercise to perform. Some of these exercises are moving exercises, such as heeling at various paces, turning, circling, or stepping to one side, calling your dog to you. Others are stationary exercises, such as having your dog lie down, stay, or

pivot in heel position. You can talk to your dog throughout and repeat commands, but you can't pull him along on his leash or touch him. Points are deducted for mistakes, but scoring is not as rigorous as in traditional obedience, emphasizing teamwork more than precision. Rally is a great way to get involved in obedience sports because it's fairly low-key and a lot of fun!

Each exercise has a particular sign with symbols that describe it, and each exercise has a particular way it should be performed. To find out more and see signs, go to *www.rallyobedience.com*.

To earn a title, a dog must qualify three times at that level. The most advanced title, Rally Advanced Excellent (RAE), is awarded to dogs that qualify ten times in both the Advanced class and the Excellent class at the same trial.

Obedience

If you and your Dachshund are more the precision types, you may prefer traditional obedience. In these trials you can't talk or gesture to your dog except to give commands, and can praise only between exercises. Instead of following printed directions, a judge tells you what to do as you go along. You get few, if any, second chances, and precision counts.

The Novice level consists of heeling on and off leash, standing off lead without moving while the judge touches him, waiting for you to call and then coming, staying in a sit position for one minute, and then a down position for three minutes. If your dog passes three times, he earns the Companion Dog (CD) title.

Open and Utility levels add jumping, retrieving, and scent discrimination, among other more challenging exercises, and dogs that qualify earn the Companion Dog Excellent (CDX) and Utility Dog (UD) titles, respectively. The Utility Dog Excellent (UDX) title is awarded for qualifying in both Open and Utility classes on the same day at ten trials, and the Obedience Trial Champion (OTCH) title is awarded to dogs that earn extremely high scores, beating other dogs in their class, in many competitions. The first hound in history to achieve this title was a Dachshund! High in Trial (HIT) is awarded to the top scorer of the day at an obedience trial.

Agility

If your Dachshund likes to run, jump, and balance, check out agility, the sport for adrenaline addicts. It's an obstacle course for dogs run against the clock, combining jumping, climbing, weaving, running, zipping through tunnels, and is loads of fun!

Several organizations, including the AKC, the United Kennel Club (UKC), the North American Dog Agility Council (NADAC), and the United States Dog Agility Association (USDAA), sponsor trials and award titles, each with slightly different styles of agility. Typical obstacles include jumps, tunnels, an elevated walk, a tall A-frame, and a teeter-totter.

AKC agility is divided into two types of courses. The Standard course includes all the obstacle types. The Jumpers With Weaves (JWW) course includes only jumps, tunnels, and weaves, usually in a somewhat more intricate course pattern than the Standard.

Of course, not all dogs jump the same heights. Dachshunds compete in either the 8-inch jump height division, for dogs 10 inches and under at the withers (top of shoulders), or in the 12-inch division, for dogs 10 to 14 inches at the withers. If this seems too high for your dog, you can enter the Preferred classes, in which the jump heights in each division are 4 inches lower. Titles earned in these classes are the same as regular titles but end in a *P*.

Conformation Competition

Do you watch the Westminster Kennel Club dog show and envision you and your Dachshund parading around a similar ring? The truth is that unless your Dachshund came from a pedigree of show dogs, with Champions (designated by a *Ch* in front of their names) within the first two generations, the chances are that he may not have the breeding required to meet the exacting points of the Dachshund standard (page 155). If your dog's breeder doesn't compete in dog shows, she probably did not choose your dog's parents with an eye toward producing a show dog. If, however, the breeder does compete in shows, ask her opinion of whether she thinks your dog has the conformation to be competitive.

Your Dachshund may have been neutered or spayed, or sold to you with a Limited Registration, all of which would render your dog ineligible for conformation showing. The breeder is the only one who can change the Limited Registration to regular registration, so her opinion is once again the first one you should seek.

You will also need to learn how to present your Dachshund in the show ring. Often a local kennel club, which you can locate through the AKC, will sponsor conformation classes. You can practice posing your dog at home by placing his front legs roughly parallel to each other and perpendicular to the ground, and his rear legs also parallel to one another with the hocks (the area from the rear ankle to the foot) perpendicular to the ground. Dachshunds are posed on a grooming table for the judge to examine, and on the floor in a lineup with the other dogs. Practice having him trot alertly in a straight line. More important than getting everything perfect is doing it all with a happy attitude, and you help him keep this merry outlook through liberal handouts of treats.

Becoming a Champion

At a show, a judge will evaluate your Dachshund in regards to type—that is, how well he exemplifies the areas of the standard that define a Dachshund as a Dachshund, areas such as head shape, coat, and overall proportions. He will also be evaluated on soundness, his ability to walk or trot in as efficient a manner as possible. Finally, he'll be evaluated on temperament, checking that he is not shy, aggressive, nor sulking. If he ranks high in comparison to his competition, he may win from one to five points toward his championship, depending on how many dogs he's defeated.

Most other breeds compete for Best of Breed instead of Best of Variety, but Dachshunds compete for Best of Breed only at independent Dachshund specialties, which are shows held only for Dachshunds. In that case the three variety winners compete against one another for Best of Breed.

Whatever the competition, even if you leave ribbonless, you'll have lots of company; just don't let your Dachshund know, and make sure you enjoy the day for what it should be: a fun outing with your dog where you can meet other Dachshund lovers.

Leash Training

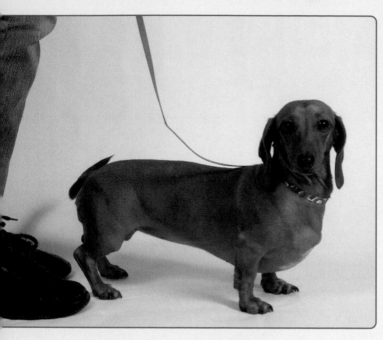

1 Place a leash on the puppy, and without pulling on it, lure him forward a step or two with a treat. Give him the treat. Keep luring him forward a little more and more as you walk slowly along with him at your side, giving him the treat every few steps.

2 If he wants to go in a different direction, let him lead for a few steps before trying to lure him along again.

3 If he refuses to move, pick him up and carry him away a few steps, then put him down and start over.

4 If he pulls ahead on the leash, dragging you, just stop. Only when he lets the leash go slack do you say "Good!" and reward or move forward.

The *Sit* Command

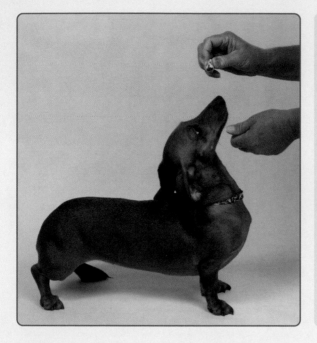

1 With him sitting with his back to a corner, hold a treat just above and behind the level of his eyes. If he bends his knees and points his nose up, say "Good!" and give him the treat.

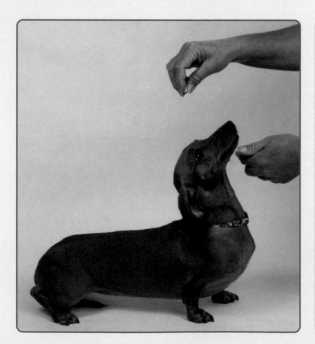

2 The next time, move the treat farther back so he has to bend his legs more to get it. Keep repeating and moving it back until he's sitting. Be sure to tell him "Good" right away and give him the treat each time.

3 Now guide him using just your hand with no treat. When he sits, give him a treat from your other hand.

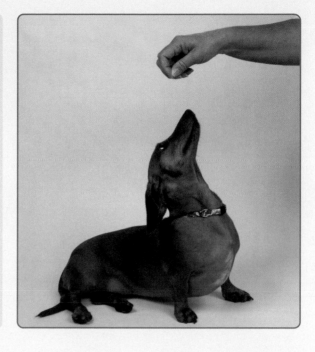

4 Gradually abbreviate your hand movements until you are only using a small hand signal. Then add a verbal signal, "Sit!" right before the hand signal. Keep practicing and rewarding him.

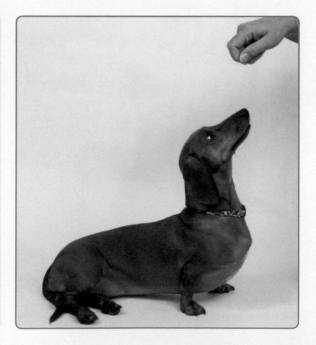

The *Stay* Command

1 Have him sit beside you, then say "Stay" while holding your palm in a "stop" signal in front of his face. If he gets up, simply put him back in position and start over, decreasing the duration you expect of him. Wait for a few seconds, then reward him and say "OK!"

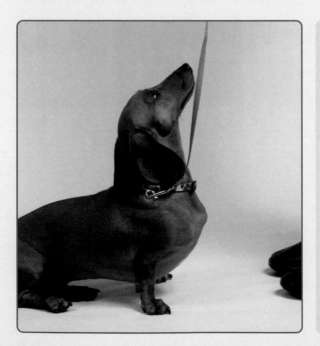

2 After he's doing this reliably, do it again, except this time, pivot so you're standing facing him. Wait for a few seconds, then reward him and say "OK!"

3 Next work on moving around so you are on either side of and even behind your dog, and then gradually increase the distance, then time.

4 Introduce mild distractions, then practice in other locations. Keep him on a long line if you're anywhere he could get loose.

Chapter Eight

Grooming a Dachshund

Whether smooth, long, or wire, the Dachshund's coat is his crowning glory, and a well-groomed Dachshund, with clean coat, short nails, and sparkling teeth, feels good about himself. And he's a pleasure to caress, cuddle, and behold.

Smooth-coat Grooming

That short sleek coat is easy maintenance, but it still does its share of shedding. Shedding occurs year-round, but tends to go through a heavy phase in the spring and fall. You can hasten shedding by giving your Dachshund a warm bath during shedding season, which seems to help any already loose hairs come out.

Your best shedding tool is a soft rubber-bristle curry brush, which tends to pull dead hair out. Use it when the hair is still damp from bathing for maximal effect, but otherwise just spend a few minutes each day running it over him.

You can also use a natural bristle brush or a horse-hair hound glove to burnish your Dachshund's smooth coat to a sheen. Spray some mink-oil coat dressing on it for a nice smell and an even shinier coat. Otherwise, there's just not much to do to it—except bathing.

Bathing

Just as your hair does, your Dachshund's hair accumulates oils that in turn attract dirt and hold odors. Your dog will have a softer, better-smelling coat with an occasional bath. Follow the steps on page 143.

Long-coat Grooming

Maintaining a long coat takes a little more effort than maintaining a short one, but it's still not very hard. Use a pin brush or comb every few days to keep the tangles out. In winter or in dry climates, spritzing the coat with

water or a coat dressing with just a tad of crème rinse in it will prevent static electricity in the coat, and keep it from becoming flyaway.

You'll probably want to bathe a long coat slightly more often than you do a smooth, but the technique is the same. Oily or dirty hair tangles and mats more easily, which is one reason mats form in oilier areas of the coat, such as behind the ears. Friction areas, such as in the armpits, are also mat magnets.

Trimming

The Dachshund is supposed to be a natural, rather than sculpted, breed, but if you really want a show-ring look, a tiny bit of trimming can help. Here's how to achieve that look:

- Use small scissors to cut around the feet so they look round and clean-cut. Cut the hair beneath the foot to the level of the foot pads.
- Use thinning shears to remove any excess hair behind the front and rear legs. This hair should be profuse, but not so much that it sticks out to the sides—or trails in everything from your yard!
- Use thinning shears to remove any fluffy hair beneath the ear so that the ear lies flatter to the head.
- Use a stripping comb to remove excessively thick hair from the sides of the neck, and along the top line from the back of the head to the tail, striving to create a smooth line.
- Use a stripping comb partway down the sides, gradually leaving the hair longer farther down the sides.

Wire-coat Grooming

The wire-coat actually takes a little more work than the other coat types, but it's still not excessive. It requires brushing only once or twice a week, and

HOME BASICS
Bathing Steps

1. Place a nonskid pad or towel in the bottom of your sink.

2. Mix up a solution of shampoo and water. It will go a lot further that way.

3. Adjust the water temperature so it would be comfortable for you to bathe in, or just a little cooler. Keep checking it throughout.

4. If possible, use a hand-held sprayer.

5. Carefully place the dog in the sink, always holding him so he can't jump out.

6. Wet him down, starting behind his ears. Save his face for last.

7. Tip: To prevent your dog from doing a wet-dog shake, keep one hand around one ear.

8. Pour or sponge the shampoo mixture onto him.

9. Work shampoo into a lather.

10. Rinse thoroughly, starting at the front and top and working toward the rear and bottom.

11. Apply a small amount of crème rinse on smooth and long coats, but not wires.

12. Rinse again.

13. Carefully place him on the floor and let him shake.

14. As soon as you let him go, he'll start running and rolling, so be careful where you want him!

15. Towel-dry him as much as possible.

16. On cold days, use a blow dryer to accelerate drying. This will take some practice, but most Dachshunds will enjoy the feel of warm (not hot!) air on their bodies.

17. Never place a dog in a closed crate with a hot dryer aimed inside and then leave him. Dogs have overheated and died that way.

bathing even less often than the other types. When bathing, use a shampoo formulated for coarse coats, and forgo the crème rinse.

It's the plucking that takes time. Left to its own, the wire coat tends to grow without shedding, until it's long, dry, and unruly. You can either hand-pluck or use a stripping comb to remove the dead parts of the coat, giving your Dachshund a dapper look. You can also use a clipper, as long as you don't intend to show him in conformation shows. Clipping is easiest, but it ruins the texture and color of the coat, leaving it softer and less bright than it would be if plucked or stripped. If you use a #7 blade, it will leave the hair fairly long and keep the general desired look. Grooming shops will clip your Dachshund, but won't pluck or strip him, as it takes too much time.

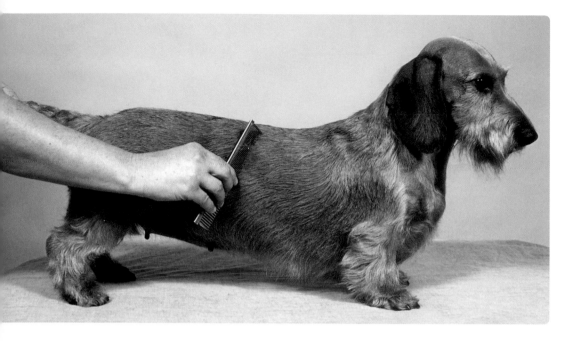

If you do want to pluck or strip your dog, the best place to learn is from your breeder. But here's a quick-start guide.

To hand-pluck, just use your thumb and index finger to grasp very few hairs at a time, and give them a slight yank. If they're ready to come out, they will. If not, they'll stay. You can get a better grip on them if you dust the coat with grooming chalk first, or if the hair is dirty.

To use a stripping comb, hold the skin taut in the area you are grooming, hold a small amount of hair between the tool and your thumb, and quickly yank the comb straight backward in the direction of hair growth.

1. Pluck or strip the hair so it's fairly short over most of his body.
2. Leave the hair fairly long on his muzzle and eye-brows. The beard should get gradually longer and fuller as it approaches the end of the muzzle. The brows, too, should get gradually shorter as they approach the outer corner of the eye. You can use scissors to taper the length.
3. Pluck or strip it short from the lip corner to the outer corner of the eye and back from there.
4. Strip it short on the top of the head, the ears, and down most of the throat and neck.
5. The hair on the legs can be longer.
6. Trim the feet as you do on the long coat.

FYI: To Remove a Mat

1. Try to pull it apart lengthwise, splitting it into two mats.
2. Keep dividing them lengthwise.
3. You can also use a mat-breaker or even a comb to comb at the edges of the mat. Remember: Comb the hair out of the mat, not the mat out of the hair!
4. For added help, first spray or saturate the mat with a tangle remover.
5. If the mat is huge, and trying to tease it out is just going to be too painful to the dog, only then should you consider cutting it out. To cut out a mat, first wriggle a comb between the mat and the skin. That way you can cut the hair beneath the mat without cutting the skin.

Skin Problems and Allergies

If your Dachshund is scratching, chewing, rubbing, and licking, he may have allergies, perhaps to inhaled allergens, things he comes in contact with, foods, or fleas. Unlike humans, in whom hay fever and other inhaled allergens typically cause sneezing, allergies in dogs more often cause itching. Signs of allergies are typically reddened, itchy skin, particularly around the ears, eyes, feet, forelegs, armpits, and abdomen. The dog may scratch and lick, and rub his torso or rump on furniture or rugs.

Allergens can be isolated with a skin test in which small amounts of allergen extracts are injected under the skin, which is then monitored for reactions. Besides avoiding allergens, some treatments are available.

The most common inhaled allergens are dander, pollen, dust, and mold. They are often seasonal. Signs most commonly appear between one and three years of age. Treatment includes antihistamines, glucocorticoids, and hypo-sensitization.

The most common allergy among all dogs is flea allergy dermatitis (FAD), which is an allergic reaction to the saliva that a flea injects under the skin whenever it feeds. It causes intense itching not only in that area, but all over the dog, especially around the rump, legs, and paws. Even a single flea bite can cause severe reactions in allergic dogs. The cure? Get rid of fleas.

FYI: Flea Treatments

Ingredient	Application	Action
Imidacloprid	Spot-on, 1–3 months	Kills 98% fleas in 1 hour; continues for 1 month
Fipronil	Spray, spot-on, 1–3 months	Kills fleas, and to a lesser extent, ticks for 1–3 months
Lufenuron	Pill, monthly	Renders fleas that bite the dog effectively sterile
Pyriproxifen	Spray, every 3 months	Renders fleas that bite the dog sterile
Selamectin	Spot-on, monthly	Kills fleas; prevents heartworms
Nitenpyram	Pill, as needed	Kills fleas in 30 minutes; no residual action
Metaflumizone	Spot-on, monthly	Kills fleas in 48 hours; continues for 1 month
Amitraz	Spot-on, collar, monthly	Kills ticks for up to 1 month
Permethrin	Spray, spot-on, as needed	Kills fleas, and to a lesser extent, ticks; no residual action

Debugging Your Dachshund

Fighting fleas used to mean treating your dog, his bedding, your house, and your yard, along with daily vacuuming and flea combing. No wonder the fleas won. Now dog owners have options that are easy and effective.

The best course of action is to vary the type of flea product you use, so that fleas have less chance of becoming resistant to a product. For example, use imidacloprid one month, fipronil another, and metaflumizone another. You can also use them in conjunction with lufenuron to prevent eggs from hatching. Most of these products are available only from your veterinarian, and they cost much more than the traditional flea sprays you can buy in the grocery store. They're worth it. They're safer and more effective, and because they have residual action, you'll spend far less money in the long run.

Ticks are sticking on as pests, but they, too, are gradually being beaten by newer products. Still, the old-fashioned ways are worth knowing. If you're in tick territory, examine your dog in the tick-favored spots: on his ears, neck, and withers, and between his toes. If you find one, use a tissue to grasp it as close to the skin as possible, and pull it straight out without twisting or squeezing.

Fleas and ticks not only cause intense itching and scratching, but fleas can cause flea allergy dermatitis and tapeworms, and ticks can cause ehrlichiosis,

babesia, and Lyme disease, among others. Your veterinarian can order blood tests if these conditions are suspected.

Mites

Mites can also cause problems. Sarcoptic mites cause sarcoptic mange, an intensely itchy disorder that you can catch. In dogs, it's often characterized by small bumps and crusts on the ear tips, abdomen, elbows, and hocks. The condition can be treated with repeated shampoos or with an injection.

CAUTION

Lyme Disease

A vaccination is available for Lyme disease, but it's not advisable for dogs that don't live in Lyme-endemic areas. Ask your veterinarian.

Demodex mites cause demodectic mange, a noncontagious but often difficult-to-treat condition. A couple of small patches in a puppy are commonplace and will usually go away on their own, but many such patches or a generalized condition must be treated with repeated dips or with drug therapy. Cases involving the feet can be especially difficult to cure.

Ear Care

Like all dogs, the Dachshund's ear canal is made up of an initial long vertical segment with an abrupt right-angle turn before reaching the eardrum. And as in all dogs, this design means that moisture and debris can accumulate in that hidden area and cause problems.

More harm is done by overzealous cleaning than by no cleaning at all. But if your Dachshund has gobs of debris, clean it using an ear cleanser from your veterinarian. Go outdoors, quickly squeeze the cleaner in the ear canal, and gently massage the liquid downward and squish it around. Then stand back and let him shake his head, flinging the sludge all over the place. Don't try this if the ear is red, swollen, or painful; these call for veterinary attention.

Ear problems are often signaled by head tilt, head shaking, scratching, inflammation, discharge, debris, or even circling to one side. They could be caused by infections, allergies, seborrhea, foreign bodies, or ear mites.

Ear mites are especially common in youngsters. They're contagious, so separate a dog you suspect of having them from other pets. Signs are head shaking, head tilt, and a dark coffee-ground-like buildup in the ears. They itch like mad, so you need to get right to them. Your veterinarian can prescribe ear drops or newer drug therapies.

The Pedicure

An important part of your Dachshund's beauty treatment is actually also an important health precaution. Nails that grow too long can get caught in carpet loops and pulled from the nail bed, and impact the ground with every step, displacing the normal position of the toes and causing discomfort, splaying, and even lameness. If dew claws, those rudimentary "thumbs" on the wrists, are present, they are especially prone to getting caught on things and ripped out, and can even grow in a loop and back into the leg. Unfortunately, some Dachshunds seem to think you're cutting not only their nails off, but their toes. You have to convince them from the time they are puppies that this is worth the treats you will be heaping on them for every nail cut.

Use nail clippers—the guillotine type are usually easier—and be sure they are sharp. Dull clippers crush the nail and hurt. You can also use a tiny nail grinder, but don't let the heat build up, and don't let any long hair wrap around the shaft. To avoid this put an old nylon stocking over the foot and push each nail through it before filing.

It's easiest to hold your Dachshund on his back in your lap to cut his nails. This allows you to better see the quick, the sensitive and potentially bleeding part of the nail. If you look under the nail, you can see where the nail begins to get hollow; anywhere it looks hollow is quickless. In this same area the nail will suddenly get much thinner.

In a light-colored nail you can see a redder area that indicates the blood supply; the sensitive quick extends slightly farther down the nail than the blood supply. When in doubt, cut too little and gradually whittle your way higher. If you cut the quick, apply styptic powder to quell the bleeding and lots of extra treats to assuage your guilt!

Dental Care

Dachshunds shed their baby (deciduous) teeth between four and seven months of age. Sometimes some of them don't fall out and the permanent teeth grow in alongside them. That's not uncommon for a few days, but if it persists for a week or more, ask your veterinarian if it may have to be extracted.

Dental care begins in puppyhood. You can use a soft-bristle toothbrush and meat-flavored doggy toothpaste. Because dogs don't spit, the foaming agents in human toothpaste can make them feel sick, and the high sodium content of baking soda is unhealthy. Brush a little, and give a treat. Make it a habit to brush once a day.

If you let plaque build up, it attracts bacteria and minerals, which harden into tartar. It spreads rootward, causing irreversible periodontal disease with tissue, bone, and tooth loss. The bacteria gain an inlet to the bloodstream, where it can cause kidney and heart valve infections.

Hard crunchy foods can help, but they won't take the place of brushing. If tartar accumulates, your Dachshund may need a thorough cleaning under anesthesia. You wouldn't think of going days, weeks, months, or even years without brushing your teeth. Why would you expect your dog to?

Breed Truths

Occlusion

A Dachshund's front teeth should meet, such that the top front teeth just barely overlap the bottom one. This is called a scissors bite. Some Dachshunds, just like some people, have poor occlusion.

- Overbite: the front top teeth are well in front of the bottom ones, so a gap is between them.
- Level bite: the top and bottom front teeth meet tip to tip.
- Underbite: the top front teeth are behind the bottom ones.
- Parrot mouth: the top jaw is much longer than the bottom one, so the top canine teeth are in front of the bottom canine teeth, which is not the norm.
- Wry mouth: the occlusion may be under on one side and over on the other.
- Base narrow: the bottom jaw is too narrow compared to the top, so that the bottom canine teeth may pierce the roof of the mouth. This often occurs along with a parrot jaw.

Chapter Nine

The Senior Dachshund

With the help of good care, good genes, and good luck, your Dachshund will be with you for many years. And one day you'll notice he's matured into a senior citizen, a time that many Dachshund owners contend is nonetheless the best time of all. But a Dachshund pensioner needs special precautions to stay healthy and happy.

Keeping Him Well up in Years

Dachshunds keep dashing even into their senior years, but don't push things. Even if he's used to jumping on and off furniture, encourage him to instead use doggy steps or a ramp. Older dogs tend to have arthritic changes that can be made worse by such stresses, and you definitely don't want to take chances with his back.

He needs exercise; you don't want your older Dachshund to just lie around (but give him a soft bed when he does). He needs low-impact exercise like walking.

He also needs mental stimulation. If he enjoys the same games he did when he was younger, great! Just be sure not to overdo them. He may prefer less strenuous activities, though. Hide treats around the room and challenge him to find them. Take him for rides in the car; just because he might not be as demanding as he used to be doesn't mean he doesn't want to go.

Long trips can be grueling for an older dog, but boarding can be stressful. Weigh carefully the pros and cons of each before deciding whether to take your older Dachshund on a long trip.

Older dogs are more susceptible to both chilling and overheating, so be sure to keep an eye on whether he's curled up and shivering or spread out and panting.

Feeding

Older Dachshunds should be fed several small meals a day. Because older dogs may have tooth loss or other dental problems, you may need to feed mushy foods. Both physical activity and metabolic rates slow in older dogs, so they tend to need fewer calories. Excessive weight can place a burden on the heart, back, and joints. However, very old dogs tend to lose weight, so at some point you may find yourself changing from trying to keep the weight off to trying to keep it on.

Most older Dachshunds don't require a special diet unless they have a special medical condition. Moderate amounts of high-quality protein are especially important for seniors.

Grooming

Older dogs lose moisture in their skin as they age, making them itchy. Regular brushing can stimulate oil production. Also consider using a moisturizing conditioner.

It's not uncommon for older dogs to have a stronger body odor than they did when younger. Search for its source. The most likely sources are the teeth, ear infections, seborrhea, or even kidney disease.

Tooth problems are very common in older Dachshunds. Bad breath, lip licking, reluctance to chew, or avoiding hands near his mouth are all signs that your dog needs veterinary dental attention. Pulling loose teeth and cleaning the remaining teeth can help your dog feel much better.

Senior Changes

Older dogs, like older people, may experience sensory or cognitive losses. Fortunately, most dogs deal surprisingly well with these changes—better, in fact, than most people do.

Vision Loss

As your dog ages, you'll start to notice a slight haziness when you look into the pupil (black part) of his eye. That's normal, and doesn't affect vision that much. However, if it becomes very gray or even white, he probably has cataracts. A canine ophthalmologist can remove the lens and even replace it with an artificial lens, just like people get.

Not all visual problems can be fixed, however. If your Dachshund loses his vision, block dangerous places, such as stairways and pools. Don't move your furniture.

Place sound and scent beacons around the house and yard so he can hear and smell where he is. Make pathways he can feel with his paws, such as carpet runners inside and gravel walks outside.

Hearing Loss

Older dogs also tend to lose their hearing. The ability to hear high-pitched sounds usually goes first, so try to call out in a lower tone of voice. Dogs can easily learn hand signals, and they can also learn to come to a flashing porch light when out in the yard. Be sure to pet your dog a lot; otherwise he must wonder why you quit talking to him.

Cognitive Loss

If you find your older Dachshund walking around aimlessly, pacing back and forth, or standing in a corner looking like he's stuck, he may be suffering from cognitive dysfunction. Basically, he's having a hard time thinking as clearly as he once did. Your veterinarian can prescribe drugs that may help him back to being his old self. You can also help by involving him in activities and small mental challenges, either through games or by teaching him new tricks.

Arthritis

Older dogs often suffer from arthritis, in which the joints become stiff and painful. You can help your arthritic dog by walking him a short distance one or more times a day. Ask your veterinarian about drugs that may help alleviate some of the symptoms, or even improve the joint.

CAUTION

Cushing's Syndrome

Older Dachshunds are particularly prone to Cushing's syndrome, or hyperadrenocorticism, in which the body produces too much of the hormone cortisol. This produces signs such as increased hunger, thirst, and urination, as well as lethargy, muscle wasting, hair loss, and especially, a pot-bellied appearance.

Your veterinarian can run some urine and blood tests to diagnose it, and can then place your dog on drugs that will help him feel much better.

Senior Health

Your older Dachshund should have a veterinary checkup twice a year. Whereas bloodwork was optional when he was younger, it's a necessity now. Standard bloodwork will tell you if he is suffering from anemia, has an elevated number of white blood cells, or has too few platelets (indicating a clotting disorder). Other tests can tell you if he has kidney failure, diabetes, liver failure, or other problems.

Because the immune system is less effective in older dogs, it's doubly important for you to shield him from infectious disease. However, if he's turned into a homebody, it may not be necessary for him to continue being vaccinated. This is an area of controversy. Ask your veterinarian about the latest guidelines.

Vomiting or diarrhea can dehydrate and debilitate an old dog quickly. They can also signal some possibly serious problems. So whereas you may have waited a day or so when he was younger, now is not the time to adopt a wait-and-see attitude.

Heart disease, kidney disease, cancer, diabetes, and Cushing's syndrome are all much more common in older dogs. Symptoms of these disorders include diarrhea, coughing, appetite changes, weight loss, abdominal distension, increased thirst and urination, and nasal discharge. Many of these disorders can be treated successfully, especially if caught early.

Chapter Ten

The Dachshund Standard

What does the ideal Dachshund look like? To most people, just like the one by their side. But to judges and serious Dachshund breeders, it's the one that best conforms to the AKC Dachshund standard. That standard is a blueprint drawn up to describe how the Dachshund should be built to do the job it was bred to do. And although a few points are included just for aesthetics, most of the points of the standard bear directly on the idea that form follows function, and function follows form.

Like most standards of German breeds, the Dachshund standard is exacting in its requirements. Of utmost importance, however, is the overall look of the dog, which the standard describes as follows: "Low to ground, long in body and short of leg, with robust muscular develop ment; the skin is elastic and pliable without excessive wrinkling. Appearing neither crippled, awkward, nor cramped in his capacity for movement, the Dachshund is well balanced with bold and confident head carriage and intelligent, alert facial expression."

Head

1. **Head:** Viewed from the side or above, the head tapers uniformly to the tip of the nose. The skull is slightly arched, and slopes gradually, with little perceptible stop into the finely formed, slightly arched muzzle, giving a Roman-nosed appearance.
2. **Eyes:** Medium size, almond shaped and dark rimmed, very dark in color.
3. **Brow:** The bones of the brow are strongly prominent.
4. **Ears:** Set near the top of the head, and rounded (not narrow, folded, or pointed). They should frame the face when the dog is at attention.
5. **Lips:** Tightly stretched, well covering the lower jaw.
6. **Nostrils:** Well open.
7. **Teeth:** Powerful canine teeth. The teeth fit together in a scissors bite.

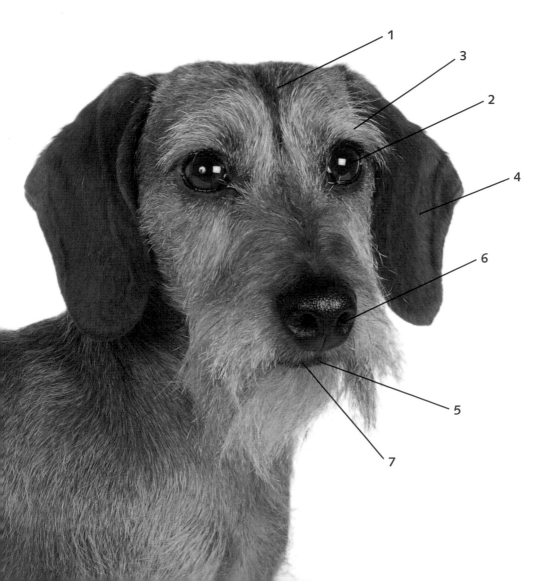

Body

1. **Neck:** Long, muscular, clean-cut, without excessive loose skin; slightly arched in the nape. Where it joins the shoulders, it should flow gracefully rather than creating an abrupt angle.
2. **Trunk:** Long and fully muscled. The back lies in the straightest possible line between the withers and the short, very slightly arched loin. A body that hangs loosely between the shoulders is a serious fault.
3. **Abdomen:** Slightly drawn up.
4. **Chest:** The breastbone is strongly prominent in front so that on either side a depression appears. The keel merges gradually into the line of the abdomen and extends well beyond the front legs. The lowest point of the breast line is covered by the front leg.
5. **Shoulder Blades:** Long, broad, and well laid back. Closely attached at the withers. Hard yet pliable muscles.
6. **Upper Arm:** Ideally the same length as, and at right angle to, the shoulder blade.
7. **Forearm:** Short, curved slightly inward.
8. **Pasterns:** Knuckling over is a disqualifying fault.
9. **Front Feet:** Front paws are tight, compact, with well-arched toes and tough, thick pads. They may tend to point somewhat outward.
10. **Hindquarters:** The pelvis, thigh, second thigh, and rear pastern are ideally the same length and give the appearance of a series of right angles.
11. **Rear Pasterns:** Short and strong, perpendicular to the second thigh.
12. **Hind Feet:** Smaller than the front paws, toes compactly closed and arched. The entire foot points straight ahead and is balanced equally on the ball and not merely on the toes.
13. **Croup:** Long, rounded, and full, sinking slightly toward the tail.
14. **Tail:** Set in continuation of the spine, extending without kinks, twists, or pronounced curvature, and not carried too high.

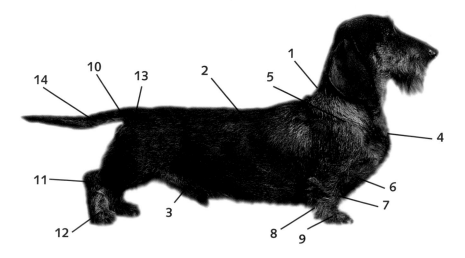

View From the Front

1. **Skull:** neither too wide nor too narrow
2. **Thorax:** appears oval and extends downward to the mid-point of the forearm.
3. **Rib Cage:** appears full and oval.
4. **Elbows:** close to the body, yet capable of free movement.
5. **Wrists:** are closer together than the shoulder joints. The inclined shoulder blades, upper arms, and curved forearms form parentheses that enclose the rib cage, creating the correct "wraparound front."

FYI: Dachshund Movement

Dachshunds in the show ring are evaluated at a trot. Here's what the judges are looking for:

- The front legs reach out in front, with a long, low stride.
- The rear legs push off behind with good power, without lifting toward the belly or appearing to walk on the rear of the hocks. Their forward equals their rear extension.
- The head should be carried fairly high, but not jutting straight up.
- The tail should be carried confidently, but not straight up.
- From the front and rear, the legs should converge slightly toward the midline with increasing speed. The front legs won't make a straight line because they may be inclined inward slightly at the wrists, but the rear legs should be a straight line (that is, the hocks should point neither in nor out).
- You should not see the front pads coming at you, but you should see the rear pads going away.

Your Dachshund won't have to conform exactly to these points just to warm your lap, chase a ball, and make you laugh, but it is fun to see how many traits he still has that hunters selected centuries ago.

The Whys of the Standard

"His hunting spirit, good nose, loud tongue and distinctive build make him well-suited for below-ground work and for beating the bush. His keen nose gives him an advantage over most other breeds for trailing." From the 2007 AKC Dachshund standard.

The Dachshund standard describes the ideal form of a dog developed to follow its quarry over varying terrain, dig into its burrow, squeeze through low passageways, confront a tenacious adversary, and drag it to the surface. To do this a dog needs to have the following characteristics:

- Open nostrils that allow for free breathing.
- Well-developed nasal passages that allow for olfactory receptors.
- Sound, efficient movement above ground.
- Shoulders set obliquely on the body, for better digging ability in close quarters.
- A wraparound front, which helps when digging in close quarters, allowing the feet to dig toward the midline and throw the dirt outward. Such a front also distributes weight toward the midline when trotting, preventing the dog from swaying back and forth inefficiently.
- Short legs, to allow the dog to fit in small places.
- Sloping pasterns to allow for better cushioning when moving, and for better digging leverage. Knuckling over, in which the wrist joints are in front of the wrists, causes a very unstable front and is a disqualifying fault.

Fun Facts

Do Dachshunds have extra vertebrae?

Some people think Dachshunds must have more vertebrae (backbones) than other dogs to explain their length. But even though it could be said that Dachshunds have more backbone than the average dog, they have the same number of backbones. It's their dwarfed legs on a normal-sized, but slender, body that makes them appear so long, along with a slight lengthening of each individual vertebra.

- An abrupt angle between shoulders and upper arm, to allow the dog to fold its limbs and crawl.
- Strong body, to provide the muscle power and weight needed to over-power quarry.
- A strong, arched neck for hanging on to the quarry.
- Strong underjaw for better grasping power.
- Fairly wide skull behind the eyes, which is where the jaw muscles traverse to attach to the top of the skull.
- Scissors bite, with well-developed canines, for better grasping and biting ability.

Temperament According to the Standard

As important as structure is for a hunting dog, temperament is even more important. The AKC Dachshund standard states: "The Dachshund is clever, lively and courageous to the point of rashness, persevering in above- and below-ground work, with all the senses well developed. Any display of shyness is a serious fault."

A nervous, shy, shivering Dachshund is probably not up to exploring the wilds for game or to facing a fierce badger; however, an overly aggressive Dachshund is equally incorrect. The hunting Dachshund is expected to get along with other people and dogs on the hunt. He need not be outgoing to them, but he must be amiable and tolerant.

Dachshund Resources

Organizations

All-breed
American Kennel Club
www.akc.org

Canadian Kennel Club
www.ckc.ca

United Kennel Club
www.ukcdogs.com

Dachshund
Dachshund Club of America
www.dachshund-dca.org
(This site also links to international
and local Dachshund clubs.)

North American Teckel Club
www.teckelclub.org

National Miniature Dachshund Club
http://dachshund-nmdc.org

Health and Research
Dachshund Orthopedic Disc Group
    E-mail Resource
www.dodgerslist.com

Disabled Dachshund Society
www.ourdds.org

AKC Canine Health Foundation
www.akcchf.org

Morris Animal Foundation
www.morrisanimalfoundation.org

Web Pages
Dachshund.org
www.dachshund.org

Dachshund Circus
www.dachshundcircus.com

The Dachshund Network
http://thedachshundnetwork.com

For the Love of Dachsies
www.dachsie.org

Index

THE TEAM BEHIND THE *TRAIN YOUR DOG* DVD

Host **Nicole Wilde** is a certified Pet Dog Trainer and internationally recognized author and lecturer. Her books include *So You Want to be a Dog Trainer* and *Help for Your Fearful Dog* (Phantom Publishing). In addition to working with dogs, Nicole has been working with wolves and wolf hybrids for over fifteen years and is considered an expert in the field.

Host **Laura Bourhenne** is a Professional Member of the Association of Pet Dog Trainers, and holds a degree in Exotic Animal Training. She has trained many species of animals including several species of primates, birds of prey, and many more. Laura is striving to enrich the lives of pets by training and educating the people they live with.

Director **Leo Zahn** is an award winning director/cinematographer/editor of television commercials, movies, and documentaries. He has directed and edited more than a dozen instructional DVDs through the Picture Company, a subsidiary of Picture Palace, Inc., based in Los Angeles.